mega makers!

Holiday club programme

for 5- to 11- year olds

© Scripture Union 2013
First published 2013
ISBN 978 1 84427 786 5

Scripture Union
207–209 Queensway, Bletchley, Milton Keynes, MK2 2EB
Email: info@scriptureunion.org.uk
Website: www.scriptureunion.org.uk

British Library Cataloguing-in-Publication Data
A catalogue record of this book is available from the British Library.

Printed and bound in India by Nutech Print Services India

Cover and internal design: kwgraphicdesign
Cover and internal illustrations: Sean Parkes

Main contributor: Ro Willoughby
Additional material by Alex Taylor, Sarah Bingham
and Kay Morgan-Gurr

Scripture Union is an international Christian charity working with churches in more than 130 countries.

Thank you for purchasing this book. Any profits from this book support SU in England and Wales to bring the good news of Jesus Christ to children, young people and families and to enable them to meet God through the Bible and prayer.

Find out more about our work and how you can get involved at:
- www.scriptureunion.org.uk (England and Wales)
- www.suscotland.org.uk (Scotland)
- www.suni.co.uk (Northern Ireland)
- www.scriptureunion.org (USA)
- www.su.org.au (Australia)

Contents

The mega invention

Mega Makers! is a seven-day children's holiday club: an opening Sunday service, five club sessions and a closing Sunday service. The focal point of this club is the Mega Machine which has been invented by the main presenter supported by his apprentice. This machine has the ability to enlarge anything that is placed inside it and after the final testing at the club will be released onto an unsuspecting world. The Mega Machine demonstrates the concept of things getting bigger and bigger which parallels the theme of **Mega Makers!** that the more we discover about God, the vaster his love for us may seem. This calls us to respond by loving him and becoming lifelong followers of Jesus.

Mega Makers! resource book

This resource book is packed with creative ideas on how to explore these stories from the life of Jesus – ideas you can change and adapt to suit your club and context. There are also ideas for construction (craft), games, drama, creative prayer and worship. **Mega Makers!** has a mixture of up-front presentation and small-group activities, allowing children and leaders to build meaningful relationships with each other and with God.

The holiday club programme is written for the 5 to 11 age group. There are ideas on the **Mega Makers!** website at www.scriptureunion.org.uk/megamakers for extending the age group to include under-5s and/or 11 to 14s. It is for you to decide the best age group for your club, and select the activities to fit.

Every effort has been made to ensure this programme is suitable for children with little or no church background. It is a tool for churches whose desire is to reach out to children and their families outside their church community. It should work equally well for churches wishing to use it as a discipleship resource for children already part of the church family.

Mega Makers! DVD

Children's author and storyteller Bob Hartman and former CBBC presenter Gemma Hunt will bring the stories from Matthew's Gospel alive in stunning settings such as The Eden Project and The Deep, as well as exploring God's most amazing invention: the natural world! The land and sea, the plants and the creatures, and most incredibly each of us!

The DVD also contains the **Mega Makers!** song, backing tracks, training material on leading small groups and additional resources.

Inventor's Notebook

This 48-page booklet contains all the key Bible text taken from the Contemporary English Version, along with small-group material, puzzles and extra information. It is ideal for use with 8 to 11s. *Inventor's Sheets* for under-8s are also available in this book and can be found in the Mega toolkit section at the end of the book (as well as on the DVD and website). There is guidance on how to use both these resources as part of the small-group time in each day's programme, and on page 11. Both *Inventor's Notebook* and *Inventor's Sheets* help maintain contact with children's homes and act as a reminder, in the weeks after the club, of what the children experienced at **Mega Makers!**. You can buy *Inventor's Notebook* as multiple copies – see the inside cover for details.

More information on these and other resources can be found on the inside front cover. For all details of the publicity materials produced by CPO, see the inside back cover. (Please note, CPO resources are not available through Scripture Union.)

Mega Makers! terminology

Boffin and Brainwave

The main presenters of **Mega Makers!** Boffin is the inventor of the Mega Machine and Brainwave is his apprentice. They guide children through the session, introducing the different elements and delivering some of the teaching for the day.

The Mega Machine

What your Mega Machine looks like depends entirely on the space available and the imagination of your team. The only essential components are an entrance into which objects can be inserted in some way, and an exit for the enlarged objects to be ejected. You will find some suggestions on the **Mega Makers!** website.

The Storyteller

Different people can tell the story each day using the script and suggestions for visual aids. A different method of storytelling, which will aid the memory and enable children to share the story with others when they get home, is suggested for each story.

Toolsheds

These are the small groups that the children are part of throughout the club. In these groups, children will explore the Bible, have their refreshments, pray together, and do games and construction.

Mechanics

The children at **Mega Makers!**

Engineers and Junior Engineers

These are the leaders of each Toolshed and those helping them. The Engineer not only has responsibility for the children in the Toolshed but will also be supporting the Junior Engineers, who may never have been involved in a holiday club before or may be someone who could be a leader at next year's club.

Innovation

The music group.

Elastic Eureka

Leads the stretch inventions warm-up and maybe the games too.

NB A fuller description of each of these roles can be found on pages 18 to 21.

Visit the Mega Makers! website

To access downloadable versions of the photocopiable resources and other useful material, go to www.scriptureunion.org.uk/megamakers. You can also read about other people's experiences and check out the advice given by other users on the message boards.

INTRODUCING **MEGA MAKERS!**

Project programme

THE AIMS OF MEGA MAKERS!

The overall truth we want children to explore at **Mega Makers!** is that God's love for them is vast – far wider and longer and higher and deeper than they can ever imagine. The more we discover about his love, the bigger and bigger it seems. Jesus' life, death and resurrection are the ultimate expression of God's love for us. The seven stories in **Mega Makers!** from Matthew's Gospel focus on what it means to be a lifelong follower of Jesus, enabling children to make a response to the God whose love gets 'vaster and vaster'.

Aims
- To demonstrate to children by word and action that God's love for them is vast
- To hear the stories from Matthew's Gospel about how Jesus called people to follow him
- To invite children to respond to God's love by becoming lifelong followers of Jesus, and to enable children who are already in a relationship with him to grow in their faith and understanding
- To offer a safe and fun environment for all the children
- To encourage the growth of Christian faith in all the adults who are involved in the club, whether team members or parents/carers who may be on the premises for the very first time

THEME AND SETTING

Mega Makers! centres around the Mega Machine, which is an invention where small items are put in and larger items come out. In this way, it reflects the themes drawn out of the Bible passages of things getting bigger, wider, deeper and greater. **Mega Makers!** could have a very simple setting or could be as sophisticated as you wish! For example, you could set **Mega Makers!** around an inventor's workshop, with all the scope for mad designs and equipment that are associated with an inventor. Alternatively, the environment could just include the Mega Machine in the alltogether part of your meeting area, as grand and quirky as you choose to make it.

The inventions theme is picked up in several different ways:
- The club is introduced and led by Boffin and Brainwave, an inventor and his apprentice.
- The children are called Mechanics and are led by Engineers.
- There are other invention-related games and activities.

For more ideas and information on setting up your venue, see page 17.

TEACHING PROGRAMME

The Sunday services begin with the start of Jesus' ministry in Matthew's Gospel (chapter 3) with the mission of John the Baptist and conclude with Jesus' great commission (chapter 28). Sandwiched between them are the five Bible stories of the club sessions.

* RT France's *The Gospel of Matthew* in the NOCNT series of Bible commentaries (Eerdmans) has been a wonderfully insightful resource in the writing of this programme.

In Jesus' ministry there are many things we could describe as getting bigger, wider, deeper and greater. We will discover these as we look at Matthew's Gospel. Each of the four Gospel writers presented the life of Jesus from their own distinct angle.* Matthew's account is well-constructed but sometimes the different Gospel accounts are hard to fit together so it is important that in using **Mega Makers!** you stick to Matthew's version. This is especially so when we read the resurrection stories on Day 5.

Matthew places great emphasis on how Jesus calls people to follow him. What we long for most in running a holiday club is that as a result boys and girls will become lifelong followers of Jesus, and that everyone associated with the club will grow in their love for and understanding of our 'great big God'.

Presenting the Bible story

When you come to the Bible story each day think carefully about how to present it. The **Mega Makers!** DVD can be used on its own or alongside your method of storytelling. We have provided a basic script for each day which you can follow but there is scope for the storyteller to adapt to their own style and the circumstances of the club. A different method of storytelling, which will aid the memory and enable children to share the story with others when they get home, is suggested for each story.

Methods of storytelling:
Day 1 – child participation and props
Day 2 – miming team members
Day 3 – eight dramatic actions
Day 4 – visual aids
Day 5 – a story bag

These 'tools' are sometimes referred to in the Bible discovery time so if you are not going to use these suggestions, you will need to adapt the material used in the Toolsheds.

(There is an excellent training feature on storytelling available as a paid-for download on the **Mega Makers!** website at www.scriptureunion.org.uk/megamakers.)

Mega Makers! covers seven days; five days of holiday club and a Sunday service at the start and the end. If you don't want to run for the full seven days, the **Mega Makers!** website has a document on how to adapt the material for three or four days.

Sunday service 1
Louder and louder – the message of Jesus

Key passage Matthew 3:1–17; 4:17

Key storylines
- John the Baptist bursts onto the scene, calling people to turn back to God.
- John baptises Jesus in the River Jordan.
- Jesus himself then begins to preach the same message with the invitation to turn back to God. This message is getting louder and louder!

Key aims
- To hear how John the Baptist came to announce that Jesus had come and people needed to listen to his life-changing message.
- To launch the holiday club so that church members can commit to pray for the coming week.
- To welcome any children and parents/carers coming to the club who are not usually part of the worshipping community.

Day 1
Wider and wider – the invitation to follow Jesus

Key passage Matthew 9:9–13

Key storylines
- Jesus invited Matthew, the disliked tax collector, to follow him.
- Matthew later invited Jesus to have dinner with him and his friends and acquaintances. This meant that Jesus met some of the unsavoury characters Matthew associated with.
- The Mega Machine 'receives' small bread rolls and spits out huge loaves of bread.

Key aims
- To welcome each child to the club, setting the tone for the next few days.
- To help children grasp that Jesus' invitation started with a few people but was spread wider and wider, to all sorts of people, of all ages and included those who were unpopular.
- From the start, plant the truth that Jesus invites everyone at **Mega Makers!** to follow him, whatever they are like, whatever their background. His invitation is offered to a wider and wider group of people.
- To enable children to see the vastness of God's love for them.

Day 2
Deeper and deeper – the trust in Jesus

Key passage Matthew 8:23–27

Key storylines
- Matthew tells the story of Jesus getting into the boat and the disciples follow him, drawing out what it means to be a follower of Jesus.
- As the storm rages, the disciples call upon the sleeping Jesus who, after challenging them about their lack of trust in him, calms the storm. Shocked, the disciples wonder just who Jesus is.
- The Mega Machine is not working properly. In frustration Brainwave throws his drink into it and out comes a bucketful of water.

Key aims
- To welcome each child back to the club.
- To help children grasp that being a follower of Jesus means that our trust in him will get deeper and deeper. This can mean enjoying being with Jesus, but in tough times it means we learn to trust him more.
- To discover more about Jesus as a person, how he has control over creation, the world he himself made.
- To enable children to see the increasing depth of God's love for them.

Day 3
Stronger and stronger – the power of Jesus

Key passage Matthew 9:18,19,23–26

Key storylines
- A leader of the synagogue exercises great faith in coming to Jesus and asks him to come and simply touch his daughter who has died. We don't know why or how this man has such faith in Jesus, but he obviously trusts that Jesus' power can make her live. His faith is rewarded.
- The Mega Machine is not ejecting the enlarged objects with enough power so Boffin decides to make some adjustments to increase the power of expulsion.

Key aims
- To welcome each child back to the club.
- To explore the different meanings of the word 'power' and how Jesus' power is not about physical force but is to do with enabling God to make a difference to people's lives. This is an inner power.
- To help children grasp that being a follower of

Jesus means that we want God to give us the power to understand, know and follow him.
- To discover more about Jesus as a person, how his power brought a girl back to life again – and two years later, God's power, which is stronger and stronger, would bring Jesus to life again in a completely new way.
- To enable children to see the increasing depth of God's love for them.

Day 4
Greater and greater – the love of Jesus

Key passage Matthew 26:36–41,50b,56b; 27:27–46,50,54

Key storylines
- Matthew's retelling of the crucifixion makes it clear that his death was not the end.
- Boffin and Brainwave disagree over what to put in the Machine. Brainwave is so frustrated that he loses his temper. But he comes to realise that Boffin loves him and wants the best for him which is why Boffin puts up with him.

Key aims
- To welcome each child back to the club.
- To help children engage with the story of the crucifixion, seeing how much Jesus suffered but also how he was not a victim to feel sorry for. He chose to die because he loves us. We can understand how his love is greater than we can ever imagine!
- To challenge children to become lifelong followers of Jesus.
- To enable children to see the increasing depth of God's love for them – it is **greater and greater**.

Day 5
For ever and ever – friendship with Jesus

Key passage Matthew 28:1-10

Key storylines
- Matthew's retelling of Jesus' appearance to the women with four component parts – an earthquake; the angel comes from heaven and removes the stone to reveal that the tomb is empty; the impact this has on the guards; the women meeting Jesus on their way from the tomb.
- Boffin and Brainwave find it hard to believe that the Machine is now working. They put two things into the Machine which come out larger. Such success is worth a

celebration. So they don party hats, balloons and organise a party.

Key aims

- To welcome each child back to the club and to give them a memorable final day.
- To help children engage with the story of the resurrection, seeing how dramatic it was that Jesus came alive again. This means that he is alive with us today.
- To awaken children to the call to tell others that Jesus is alive, just as Jesus told the women to tell the other followers.
- To challenge children to become lifelong followers of Jesus. Friendship with him goes on for ever and ever.
- To enable children to see the increasing depth of God's love for them.

Sunday service 2
More and more – the followers of Jesus

Key passage Matthew 28:16–20

Key storylines

- Jesus has come alive again and over the next 40 days appeared several times to his disciples.
- At this meeting on a mountain Jesus gives his disciples a challenge to go all over the world teaching others about him, so that they too could become followers of Jesus.

Key aims

- To hear about and reflect on the challenge Jesus gave (and gives) to those who follow him so that more and more people could become followers.
- To share with the rest of the church family what has been happening in the holiday club.
- To welcome any children and parents/carers who have been part of the club but do not usually come to worship.

PROGRAMME BREAKDOWN

Each day's programme contains the following elements:

Team preparation

Any holiday club's success is built on prayer. This material provides notes to encourage the team to think and reflect personally on each day's Bible story from Matthew. Before the children arrive, spend some time digging into the Bible story. Pray for each other and pray for the children in your club.

During this time, you'll also need to check that you have everything you need for the session (the equipment checklist for each day is a useful way of doing this), make health and safety checks and ensure everything and everyone is ready for the children's arrival.

Arriving at Mega Makers!

The first moments at **Mega Makers!** are so important! Be welcoming, but not overwhelming, in putting the children and accompanying adults at their ease. Strike a balance between helping parents to see that their children will be safe with you and giving children a sense of the fun that they'll have during the session. Make sure you have enough people at the registration desk (especially on the first day) to show children and their parents to the right groups. It's always helpful to have someone available to answer questions as the parents leave, or to remind them of the collection time, or just to say a cheerful, 'See you later!'

Registration

Make sure that the registration desk is well organised with spare forms and pens for any parents who want to register their children at the door. Have a floor plan of your venue to show where each team is sited, so that parents can find their way round. If possible, have a large plan available a little distance away from the desk so that parents dropping children at more than one group can go back to check the layout without clogging up the registration area. Ensure parents have filled in a collection slip so you know who will be picking the child up at the end of the session. Collection slips and registration forms are available on the **Mega Makers!** website.

Clocking in

This time is not just a fill-in until the last child arrives. During this time the key aims will be relationship-building and feedback. It is a great time to check out who can remember the Learn and remember verse or the story from previous days. Each day, the children will be encouraged to create their own mini-machines in their Toolsheds during this time, if there is space – see page 17 for suggestions. But there is also a suggested introductory activity to do as children arrive. These build on the theme and allow you plenty of time to chat and get to know each other better. Children could bring their own inventions or information about their favourite inventor. If the Toolsheds are named after different inventors, each group could learn facts about their specific inventor and share what they've learnt in the all-together time. Any child with jokes, pictures, messages or questions should place them in the Brainbox as they arrive.

Inventor's workshop

This section of the programme where the children are all together is designed to be fast-moving and fun. It is led from the front by the inventor and his apprentice – Boffin and Brainwave. It contains the main teaching for the day, together with the other elements outlined below.

Stretch inventions

Elastic Eureka calls three leaders or older children to the front having primed them to invent a body position which they can hold in a frozen position for 15 seconds and which is physically possible for younger children. These can be related to the theme of the day. Two leaders or children could devise a position together. Each child or pair has to attempt to copy this invented position and then hold it for 15 seconds (or longer if the children are able to sustain it). Play a stretch invention jingle while the children 'stretch'.

Mega Machine

Boffin assisted by Brainwave has been creating a Mega Machine. However your machine has been created (see page 5), on Day 1 you need to leave something incomplete, whether it is a surface that needs painting, a piece of scaffolding that needs installing, or a ladder or flag that needs to be put in place! The Mega Machine has to go through a strict series of trials, which will continue throughout the club. On Day 2 water has to shoot out of the Mega Machine, so take necessary precautions.

Messy mechanics

This is a challenge which is fast-paced and often messy, led from the front for leaders or children to take part in. Encourage children watching to volunteer their leader and to cheer on all volunteers. Each day's challenge is different and will need a person from the team to make sure all the resources are ready to use at the right moment.

Music makers

Think about the children you are running this club for. If not many are church children choose songs that don't require them to sing that they believe in God; use songs that tell about how great God is. There is one theme song which provides a soundtrack to your club, helps to develop its identity and is fun to sing. There is also a song called 'Wide and long and high and deep' to help children learn the Learn and remember verse. The audio versions for both songs are on the DVD. The sheet music and words for the theme song are on pages 88 to 90; the sheet music and words for the Learn and remember song are on the **Mega Makers!** website. You can easily devise actions to accompany both songs.

Here are some other suggested songs that would work well with the theme:

- Far up in the north
  Light for Everyone CD, SU
- God is an awesome God
  Light for Everyone CD, SU
- Taller than the mountains
  Reach Up! CD, SU
- He's got the whole world in his hands
  Junior Praise 78
- Jesus' love is very wonderful
  Junior Praise 139
- Our God is a great big God
  Songs of Fellowship 2004
- God's love is deeper
  kidsource 84

The songs from *Light for Everyone* and *Reach Up!* can be downloaded as individual tracks (for 0.79p) by going to www.scriptureunion.org.uk/shop and typing the song title into the search box on the page.

From the Maker's Manual

This is the main storytelling section of the club. A storyteller tells the day's story using various props and visual aids. The children are encouraged to take part in different ways. Although there is a script, the storyteller needs to add their own take on the story and prepare well, especially ensuring that they know how they are going to end the story.

The **Mega Makers!** DVD contains five storytelling episodes, told by Bob Hartman and Gemma Hunt, helping you tell the Bible story. If you don't have any strong storytellers, you may choose the DVD as the primary storytelling tool. Alternatively, you might choose to do the live retelling and reinforce it with the DVD. See page 5 for more details about the DVD.

Mega words

Each day has a key phrase (which is in two parts, the 'expanding words', and the subject of expansion). This will help children remember what they have learnt, and to share with others when they get home as well as keeping leaders focused on the message they want children to learn, eg 'Stronger and stronger – the power of Jesus'. There is a suggestion for how to introduce the **Mega Makers!** words each day.

Learn and remember verse

Of course, we want children to learn, understand and remember verses from the Bible and many holiday clubs reward children or groups of children who demonstrate that they have learnt the verse(s). But there is more to remembering a Bible verse than just being able to recite it. At **Mega Makers!** unpacking

Sample programme

This programme runs for 2 hours 15 minutes, not including preparation and clear up time.

ACTIVITY	RUNNING TIME	INCLUDES
Team preparation	30 minutes	Spiritual and practical preparation for the team
Clocking in (small groups)	10 minutes	Introductory activities in Toolsheds
Inventor's workshop (all together)	45 minutes	Up-front Bible teaching, DVD, stretch inventions, songs, messy game, Mega Machine, Learn and remember verse, interview
Power drill (small groups)	45 minutes	Bible discovery, refreshments, construction, games
Back to the workshop (all together)	25 minutes	Songs, drama, quiz and recap, jokes and questions, praying for the world
Clocking off (small groups)	10 minutes	Chat and finish off
Workshop clear-up	30 minutes	Team tidy, debrief and preparation for next session

Ephesians 3:18 is one of the main ways that the vastness of God's love will be explained. Each day a different part of the verse will be explained as it is set in the context of the apostle Paul writing to Christians in Ephesus. Children who learn the verse quickly can encourage others to do the same. Inventing some actions will help them. Older children could be challenged to learn verse 19 as well.

We have provided the verse from the Good News Bible but you may prefer to use the New Century Version as it is particularly clear for children to understand.

The Learn and remember verse song includes many of the words from Ephesians 3:18 but it still needs explanation. If you only use this song you will miss out on much of the core teaching which is related to the full version of Ephesians 3:18.

Ask an engineer

Children learn a lot from hearing the story of other people's lives and all team members are role models for the children. To hear a small part of a team member's journey of faith is very valuable. Whoever is interviewed needs to work hard to use language and concepts that children can relate to.

Power drill

The children move into their Toolsheds for Bible exploration, construction, games and refreshments.

You can choose to do the construction and games in each toolshed, in different age groups or all together. It depends on what team and facilities you have. Whatever you do, encourage team members to continue to build relationships with the children.

Down tools

Make sure you have refreshments that are suitable for children of other faiths. The easiest way to do this is to provide food suitable for vegetarians (ie no gelatine) and which contains no pork products. Do tell everyone that the food is OK otherwise they might assume it isn't and not have any. On Day 1 you may choose to provide bread rolls (include a gluten-free option) since bread dough expands and is featured at the start of the programme.

Bible discovery

The Engineers help the children explore the story in the Bible. Our aim is to help them to learn how to read the Bible for themselves and think about how it relates to their lives, as they read the story they have just heard. The *Inventor's Notebook* (8–11s) or the *Inventor's Sheet* (5–8s) will guide the children as they engage with the Bible. Some groups with younger children begin this time as the children enjoy their refreshments, since they are relaxed and in one place. This is often after a loo break. It can take some small children a surprisingly long time to finish eating a biscuit!

It is important to make sure that the leaders are well-prepared, which is vital if we are to fulfil our aims for the club in helping children to respond to God. If possible, provide copies of the leaders' notes that are part of the material for each session. (These can be found on the website.) Less experienced leaders would benefit from a more experienced leader going over the notes with them.

Power tool

Each day, to develop further the Bible discovery, there is a suggestion for how the group might talk with God. This is connected with the material in *Inventor's Notebook* or on the *Inventor's Sheets*. Encourage every child to join in, whether silently or out loud. Pass a small object around the group (such as something connected to the group's mini-machine, or something that suggests God giving us insight such as a torch) so that when a child holds the object they know it is their turn to speak out loud or they can simply pass the object onto the next person.

Construction

In **Mega Makers!** there is a choice of construction projects. The first five look at solving problems with simple materials and there is no take-home item. The next five items follow the themes for the day's teaching and the children will have something to take home with them. Whichever projects you choose to do, the construction time creates an environment where you can strengthen relationships, chat about the day's teaching and have fun together. The construction projects can be found in the Mega toolkit on pages 63 to 67 or for further inspiration, see *Ultimate Craft*.

Games

Games used during **Mega Makers!** can be found on pages 67 to 69. For further inspiration, see *Ultimate Games*, which contains hundreds of ideas that might be suitable for your club. Make sure you risk-assess these activities and collect all the necessary materials beforehand. The games time is another good opportunity for leaders and children to chat and build relationships.

Back to the workshop

During this time, the children are all together for activities led from the front.

Brainbox
(for jokes, pictures, messages and questions)

As children return from their Toolsheds, Boffin and Brainwave should read some of the contributions left in the Brainbox. On Day 1, Boffin should explain that the Brainbox is where the children can secretly leave their jokes, messages, pictures and questions and that, each day, some of these will be read out and shown, as well as questions answered. The Brainbox could be a miniature version of the Mega Machine with a door or very large slit cut out, through which children can post things.

Drama
Professor Ventor's Miracle Matter-Maker

Professor Ian Ventor (or Eve Entor, if played by a woman) makes eccentric machines in the style of Heath Robinson. His workshop is littered with inventions that never quite worked or have seen better days. However, he's determined to get his super-invention, the Mechanical Miracle Matter-Maker, up and running, and makes slow progress each day to do this. As well as his assistant May Kamess and his automaton called ROBOT, Ian takes on some rather dubious apprentices. One of these turns out to be a rival inventor, Dr O'Good. He is out to steal other people's ideas and wreck their inventions. On Day 4 it seems he has succeeded in his plans but ROBOT comes to the rescue and the team can at last spread the good news of the Mechanical Miracle Matter-Maker, which will change people's lives. The drama is not designed to be a primary teaching tool, but a reinforcement of the theme and a chance for some slapstick fun!

Wide, wide world

People expect Christians to pray and it is important that in the holiday club we help children to learn how to talk with God on their own and with others. Each day there is a suggestion for what you can pray about in the wider world and how you might do this.

Bench test

This is a short quiz to recap the facts of the Bible story, test the children's knowledge connected to height, depth, width etc, their memory of the **Mega Makers!** words and the teaching of the day. Questions are given for each day, but you'll need to customise them and add more of your own. Keep the style of questions varied (such as asking for a straight answer, providing a choice of two or three answers, or even using pictures for some questions). Decide whether you want to use the same method of score-keeping or use a different one each day. If using different ones, they could be related to the expansion going on each day such as a smile that is 'stretched' wider and wider or a ball on the end of a piece of string that 'falls' deeper and deeper.

Fusion finale

This wraps up the all together time with the theme song and maybe another song the children have

enjoyed. Tell children what might be happening the next day to whet their appetites and remind them about the procedure for being collected by parents and carers.

Clocking off

You could finish off anything from the club that still needs work and ensure that children have everything that they need. There is a suggestion for one activity to do while you wait for 'collectors'. Engineers should make a point of saying goodbye to each child and reminding them of the next session. Take time to engage with parents/carers as the children are collected.

Workshop clear-up

It may be that some of the team have their own children at **Mega Makers!** and are unable to stay for long when the programme ends. Try to call everyone together to check any problems, briefly reminding them of tomorrow's activities and pray for the Holy Spirit to be at work in the children.

If you have time and the facilities, the team could share lunch together to round off the day.

OTHER ELEMENTS OF MEGA MAKERS!

Services

The programme contains two services, one to start the club and one to finish. These are designed to be an integral part of the club for children. This is to help you encourage children from outside your church community and their families to come into a church service. Research shows that if you advertise the club as including the services as well as the club days (so a seven-day programme rather than a five-day one), children and families with little or no church background are more likely to attend. However, children who don't attend this first service will still find it easy to join the club on Day 1. It is also great to commission the team and get your congregation praying, but this can be done during the service before the first Sunday of **Mega Makers!** This means that the first Sunday service of the club has a clear aim (and an earlier commissioning will encourage the church to pray as you prepare, as well as when the club is taking place).

Under-5s resources

For details of resources to use with 5s and under, visit the **Mega Makers!** website. The resources follow the same Bible passages and themes as the main programme.

11 to 14s resources

For details of resources to use with 11 to 14s, visit the **Mega Makers!** website. The resources follow the same Bible passages and themes as the main programme.

14 to 18s - young leaders

Having young people help out at a holiday club is a fantastic way of discipling and training them in leadership. For training materials for use specifically with 14 to 18s in leadership, go to the **Mega Makers!** website. Remember that under 18s are still regarded as children when it comes to ensuring you have the right ratio of adults to children.

Having a shorter club

If you are planning to run your club over three or four days, rather than five, go to the **Mega Makers!** website for guidance on how to adapt the material for a shorter club.

Family activities

It is a good idea to include some events in your club for families to attend all together. This will give you a chance to meet and get to know the families of children who are coming to **Mega Makers!** Involve the whole church to organise food or run activities. Here are a few things you could try:

- **Games**: organise a family games event, using some of the games ideas from pages 67 to 69. Patent Protection and Water Tower would be particularly suitable. Families could work together, or you could pair a family from your church community with one new to the church, to help build relationships.
- **Construction**: use some of the construction ideas on pages 63 to 67 to put together a family session. Activities such as wood turning, pyrography and other more robust crafts are great for encouraging family members to work together (for instance, fathers and sons). You could combine construction and games into one event.
- **Family barbecue**: these events are always popular and can be quite simple to run! Alongside the food, you could run games or construction, or a family quiz which could include questions about the stories from Matthew (for the children).
- **Big screen events**: Explore what recent or not-so-recent children's films you could show, which may, or may not have a specifically Christian content. Provide popcorn and all the other features of a trip to the cinema.

None of these ideas are groundbreaking in themselves but, run in conjunction with the club, they can involve more of the church community, introduce the church to people with little or no previous contact, in a relaxed atmosphere, and start to build relationships.

The blueprint

PLANNING MEGA MAKERS!

Think carefully about the issues involved as you start to plan a holiday club.

What are your aims?

The broad aims of **Mega Makers!** are on page 6, but each individual holiday club will have its own specific aims. **Mega Makers!** can provide a manageable, creative and fun way of reaching out to the children of your neighbourhood with the good news of Jesus. It can provide an excellent opportunity to blow any misconceptions away and to reveal to them a God who loves them powerfully.

Here are some aims you might choose for your club:

- To attract new children to join your Sunday groups or other children's activities.
- To develop your leaders' gifts and experience.
- To present the gospel to children who've never heard it.
- To provide an opportunity for children to make an initial or further commitment to follow Jesus.
- To get to know the children in your church.
- To help children in your church to grow in faith.
- To provide a project to encourage your church to work together.
- To establish links with the children's families.
- To encourage cooperation with other churches or groups in your area.
- To launch an ongoing children's group based on the **Mega Makers!** theme.
- To give parents a break in the school holidays.

Any or all of these aims may be appropriate, but you'll have to decide what you want **Mega Makers!** to achieve in your situation. If you have several aims, you'll need to decide which are the most important. Plan to evaluate **Mega Makers!** afterwards, to see if you met your aims. Decide now how you'll do that. How will you measure success? Try the aims form on the **Mega Makers!** website or DVD and work together to decide on your aims.

The children

Once you have set your aims, you'll be able to make other key decisions such as:

Who will you invite to Mega Makers!?

- Do your aims relate to the children already involved in your church, or those outside it?
- How many children do you want to involve? If your main aim is to get to know the children better, you might need to restrict numbers. On the other hand, if you want to present the gospel to children who haven't heard it, you may want as many as possible to attend. The number of leaders you have will affect your child capacity in order to meet the required adult:child ratio.
- What age range(s) do you want to target with **Mega Makers!**? Do you want to cater for an age range that is well represented in your groups, or one that isn't? Will you be able to tailor the activities in a way that will appeal to a wide age range? **Mega Makers!** is designed for use with children between the ages of 5 and 11. See page 13 for information on where to find resources to use with other age groups.

When will you run your club, and for how long?

You'll need to fix the date for your holiday club early enough for people to take it into account when they book their holidays. It is also essential that the dates do not clash with other holiday clubs in the area, activities already booked at your premises, holidays organised by local schools, holidays/camps for local Boys' Brigade, Girls' Brigade, Cub or Brownie groups. You may also want to avoid clashing with carnivals or local events but the other option is to tie in with these events intentionally and benefit from the buzz around the local area. The summer break is the most obvious time to hold your club but you could also consider running it in a half-term holiday or the Easter holidays instead. You could also consider running your club on Sundays through the summer if your other sessions stop running but this needs careful planning. You could also run the club the same morning of the week throughout the school holidays, which could reach most children some of the time. Will you run it just in the morning or for a longer day, which will delight working parents looking for cheap childcare?

The potential leaders' availability will have the most effect on the duration of your holiday club. If most of your leaders need to take time off work, it may not be practical to run a full five-day club.

If you are planning to run your club over three or four days, rather than five, go to the **Mega Makers!** website (www.scriptureunion.org.uk/megamakers) for guidance on how to adapt the material for a shorter club.

Legal requirements

There are various legal requirements you will need to be familiar with and conform to as you prepare for your holiday club. These include having a child protection policy in place, providing adequate space in your venue, meeting adult to child ratios and insurance. To obtain up-to-date information on all of these requirements, go to 'legal requirements for running a club' on the holiday and midweek clubs downloads page.

Finances

Consider your financial resources. Work out what you need money for. Examples might include:
- craft materials
- refreshments
- materials for the scenery
- photocopying/printing costs
- hire of premises
- hire of equipment such as a video projector
- **Mega Makers!** resource books for your leaders
- resources such as the **Mega Makers!** DVD and *Inventor's Notebook*
- prizes or presents for the children

Do you need to do some fund-raising? Will you charge for children to attend **Mega Makers!**? The first child in a family could be charged, with a reduction

for subsequent children. Research shows that in many cases, making a charge for a club has no effect on the number of children who come. Indeed, some parents may value a club they have had to pay for more highly than something that is free.

Publicity

The best way to ensure you have plenty of children at your holiday club is for the event to be well publicised. There is material available from CPO to help you with this. See the inside back cover for details. Here are some things to consider:

Posters and flyers
Use these to advertise **Mega Makers!**

Letters and forms
- Send a letter or invitation card to every child/family your church has contact with.
- Give each child in your church a flyer so that they can invite a friend.
- Distribute letters to all the children in your area, maybe through the local schools. Your letter could enclose an application/registration form to be returned to you. You may also need a follow-up letter, which will enclose a consent/medical form, and perhaps a **Mega Makers!** badge.

School assemblies
You may have a local Christian schools worker, or people/parents from your church who are involved in schools ministry, or there may be church members who are teachers in the locality. If so, they could promote **Mega Makers!** in a school assembly, if the school is happy for them to do so.

Press releases
Holiday clubs provide the kind of story that local papers love to cover in the summer when news is scanty. By getting a story in the press, you'll increase the appeal of your holiday club and show that the church(es) involved are reaching out into your local community. Please mention Scripture Union in your press releases or advertising since positive publicity ultimately allows SU to develop resources like this holiday club material. If you have a good relationship with your local press, make contact in the usual way and inform them of your event. If this is something you have never considered, a press release template is available on the **Mega Makers!** website. Include your club's details and send the press release to your local paper.

Prayer cards/bookmarks
It is important to keep your church informed about the club. Prayer cards or prayer bookmarks can help church members pray before, during and

after **Mega Makers!** One church with a holiday club at the end of the summer holidays held a week of prayer just before the start of the holidays. Each weekday there was an opportunity for people to pray together about the club – in cell groups, in the school library for parents straight after dropping off children, a drop-in evening for adults on their way home from work, one lunchtime after Toddlers for those around in the daytime, after-school on Friday for parents and children.

Planning in detail

Presentation and teaching

How will you adapt the material to suit your particular age group(s)? What audio/visual aids will you need? Will you need amplification or video projection equipment? Who will be Boffin and Brainwave, tell the story, conduct the interviews, lead the drama team and music group and explain the Learn and remember verse?

Programme priorities

You may not have time to fit in all the activities that are suggested. In the Toolsheds leaders could get so engrossed in general conversation that they never start on the Bible discussions, so be sure to plan carefully. When planning, be sure to put in the essentials first – up-front Bible teaching, prayer, discussion time in groups. Then add the less vital but still important things – construction, refreshments – and finally the parts that 'fill it up' – messy game, quiz.

Music

Choose the songs for the week, and gather the musicians together to rehearse them. It's good to have a number of musicians playing a variety of instruments, but make sure there is enough stage space for other things too! Choose a few new songs and a few old favourites, including non-confessional songs, so that children are not singing words they might not believe. If you don't have musicians in your team, use backing tracks, or simply sing along to a CD/MP3.

Drama

Do you need to adapt the script to fit the number or gender of your cast members, or the limitations of your venue? How much rehearsal time will you need? How will you obtain or make the necessary props, costumes and scenery?

Training

Undertaking some basic skills and knowledge training is vital for the success of the holiday club. You should aim to have at least one session together in preparation, and you should ensure that this is more or less compulsory for team members. As part of this session, the vision and practicalities of **Mega Makers!** can also be outlined. Training is outlined on page 21.

Power drill

You'll need to think about how you are going to stage this. What you do depends on your aims and the resources you have available. Here are the options:

- Every Toolshed does the same activity on the same day. This means that only one explanation from the front is needed, and Engineers can help each other. It also means that children from one family will all discover the day's activities at the same time. However this requires a lot of resources and an activity that works for all age-groups in some shape or form. Activities which suit this format are limited.
- You set up activities for the whole week and children rotate around these activities. This means fewer resources are needed and different leaders can take responsibility for leading the same activity each day. More activities are possible but it is harder to theme each activity to the day's teaching. Engineers may have less opportunity to spend with the children in their Toolsheds. You may need specific areas dedicated to each activity and your venue may not be large enough. If you have enough team members, some could just be responsible for the activity times based on their skills.

Construction/craft

How will you acquire the necessary materials and equipment? Do you need to ask the congregation to collect particular items? A dedicated craft team can be very useful to collect the necessary materials especially in the run-up to **Mega Makers!** They can make templates and patterns for children to draw around or cut out. The craft team should make up prototypes of each craft and pass on any hints to the den leaders.

Involve local schools in amassing reusable material to use during the week (yogurt pots, glass jars, plastic bottles, travel magazines for collage etc). This actively involves people in contributing to the club before it has begun, including the children and alerts the school to the club's existence, bringing extra publicity.

Games

Consider what games you can play based on the number of children, your venue and the equipment you have. Make sure you have all the equipment you need. If planning on being outside, prepare for bad-weather alternatives.

Data protection

How will you maintain the confidentiality of the information you receive on the registration forms? Make sure you abide by the principles of the Data Protection Act. Visit dataprotectionact.org for more information including the eight principles of protecting data.

Accidents

Aim for there to be at least one person appointed as a first-aider with a current first aid certificate and access to an up-to-date first aid kit. (This is not a legal requirement but it is important to take reasonable precautions to oversee the welfare of those in your care.) The whole team should know who is responsible for first aid. You will need an accident book to record any incidents which is essential in the event of an insurance claim. The matter should be recorded, however small, along with details of the action taken. For other health and safety information visit www.rospa.com.

Fire procedures

It is essential that the whole team knows emergency procedures, including fire exits and assembly points, and where to access a telephone in case of emergency. To help with this, have a practice fire drill. Ensure you keep all fire exits clear.

Prayer team

Make sure you have a team of people committed to pray throughout the preparation and the club itself. Keep the whole church well informed too. The prayer team should keep on praying for the children in the club in the months after **Mega Makers!**

Use of the Bible

One of the aims of **Mega Makers!** is to help children explore and read the Bible for themselves. So each day in Bible discovery help children find it in the Bible or in *Inventor's Notebook* and learn to look for answers there. Use a translation that is easy for children to read (Good News Bible, Contemporary English Version, New Century Version or International Children's Bible).

Setting the scene

Choosing the right venue is important. Sometimes a community hall or school is a well-equipped, neutral venue that can be non-threatening for children and parents outside the church. However, you may wish to use this opportunity to introduce children and parents to your church building. This can also help save on the cost of hiring an alternative venue. The venue needs to have enough space for the number of children and the type of activities you are planning. You will need access to the venue before the holiday club to ensure necessary preparations can be made.

Setting up the room

The holiday club will be greatly enhanced if the area where the up-front presentation takes place can be transformed into the inventor's workshop with the Mega Machine! But in addition you can display objects connected with the workshop so that the workshop 'spills' into the whole room, such as ladders, bicycle wheels, benches on which are tools and equipment. However, these must be safely secured with nothing that puts the children at risk. All this will help to spark children's imaginations. Think creatively how you can transform your venue into an exciting place.

The stage area

The Machine will be the focal point of the presentation area from where Boffin and Brainwave can run the programme. Think about where you will do your drama and where the band will be positioned. You will also need to decide where the projection screen, for projecting song words, club logo etc should be located. A draped-off area or an attached room needs to be provided for the actors in the drama to come out of. The boundary for the stage area could be marked by a masking tape line across the floor.

Toolshed locations

The rest of the room can be divided into Toolshed locations. These could be named after colours, inventors, location in the premises or the type of mini-machine that they become. (The mini-machines could have a focus on electronics, gardening, towers, balloons, ladders, wheels, junk modelling…) Much will depend on the space you have for each Toolshed. Larger space could mean that the mini-machine is developed over the course of the club with children colouring, decorating and adding features to their machine. How inventive are your children? For example, one Toolshed in a club added decorations each day and on the second day, added a children's slide to the entrance and on the third day a tunnel as an exit. If there is only room for a table and chairs, aim to decorate all wall-space or dividers as much as possible to make the Toolsheds as distinctly unique as possible. Is everyone going to sit on the floor for most of the time together in the Toolshed? If so, provide mats, cushions and clipboards.

Fill the screen

If you are using a video projector or OHP to project the song words, for example, use a default image when it is not being used, so that the screen is never blank. Use something simple, like the **Mega Makers!** logo. The logo and other artwork are available on the DVD-ROM section of the **Mega Makers!** DVD or on the website.

PHASE 2

17

Engineer enrolment

DEVELOPING PEOPLE'S POTENTIAL

As well as being a time of great fun and development for the children attending, a holiday club is also an important time for the adults leading and helping out. Helping with a holiday club can be a big step for people in the development of their gifts and ministry.

How does a holiday club develop people's potential?

- It involves people in the church who don't usually work with children.
- It is an opportunity for people of all ages to work together in a way that may not happen at any other time of the year. (A regular comment at one holiday club from team members is, 'This is the best week of the year in church!' It's probably the most demanding and tiring too!)
- It develops people's gifts and lets them take risks.
- It discovers people's untapped gifts and enthusiasms, eg you may have amateur inventors in your congregation!
- It provides a structure for the overall leadership of the club/church to seek out and encourage people to 'have a go'. Don't rely on issuing a general plea for volunteers but look at who you have available and ask people personally, giving them good reasons why you think they could fulfil whatever task you have identified. This suggests that you believe in them and they are far more likely to agree to get involved!

AREAS OF RESPONSIBILITY

A successful holiday club requires a variety of support teams to be set up and individuals taking responsibility for different areas of the programme.

Listed below are some of the different teams you will need and some of the key roles people will need to assume before, during and after the event. However, if you are running a holiday club for the first time and only have a small team of volunteers you may not be able to fill these key roles or teams. So, we have divided the list into those roles we see as essential (indicating some extra tasks those people will need to take on) and those that are great to have, if you are blessed with a larger team.

Essential roles:
- Core planning team (could also do print and publicity)
- Overall leader (could also be responsible for security, health and safety)
- Boffin and Brainwave – the presenters
- Engineers (share out extra tasks of registration, construction, games etc)
- Refreshment person
- First-aider
- Technical manager

Optional extras:
- Printing and publicity person/team
- Security, health and safety
- Registration person/team
- The Storyteller (non-essential if you use the DVD instead)
- Additional up-front roles
- Elastic Eureka
- Assistant Engineers
- Drama team
- Innovation (the worship band)
- Construction co-ordinator
- Games co-ordinator

ESSENTIAL ROLES

Core planning team

All the helpers should be involved in planning and preparing for **Mega Makers!**, but you will need a smaller team to coordinate things and make some initial decisions. As well as the holiday club's overall leader, this should include your most experienced leaders, your minister and your children's workers.

The overall leader

The overall leader and coordinator is ideally someone who is not involved in the presentation. Their role would be to:

- Make any on-the-spot decisions such as accepting extra children at the door.
- Keep the whole programme to time, moving things on when necessary.
- Look at quality of presentation, watching out for problems such as too much banter between the team and Boffin and Brainwave.
- Watch out for children who are not joining in well and helping them to become part of things.
- Being the person to whom everyone would report in the event of a fire.
- Liaising with parents and carers; being a PR figure.

Boffin and Brainwave – the presenters

They should be confident in their roles on stage and have experience of leading a programme in a fun but flexible manner. Providing much of the slap-stick humour they also need to ensure that there is a serious element to the programme. They need to keep the programme moving and engage with the children. Boffin is a studious-looking type whereas Brainwave is a fuss pot who keeps getting things mixed up and lacks confidence in both Boffin's machine and in his ability to make anything work. Boffin may or may not interview a team member, explain the Learn and remember verse, tell the story or lead the stretch inventions. But Boffin should certainly introduce the story, do the Bench test quiz and finish off with the final word.

Engineers

Each small group needs a leader called an Engineer. The Engineer should be at the club every day and will be the person with whom the children have the most personal contact. The leader's role is to get to know the children so that they feel welcome and comfortable at **Mega Makers!** The programme is designed to give these leaders enough time in the Toolsheds to have meaningful discussions, including ones that apply the teaching programme to the children's lives.

They should coordinate all small-group activities and sit with the children in their Toolsheds during the up-front times. They should have a copy of the register, be aware of any special needs and food allergies, ensuring that children all leave safely at the end of the day's session.

Refreshment person/team

This person/team will play a vital role during the week. They will be responsible for:

- Checking with the registration team that you have no children with food allergies.
- Obtaining and preparing the refreshments for the children at the agreed time.
- Tidying up after the refreshments have been given out.

If you have a team of helpers, choose one person to coordinate the group. If you are providing anything more than a drink and a biscuit, you should have someone with a food hygiene certificate. Think about using (recyclable) disposable cups or bottles to save on washing-up time.

First-aider

Aim to have at least one member of your team with a valid first-aid certificate. If possible have assistants too – a male for the boys and a female for the girls. These people will need a current first aid certificate, and access to a first aid kit. You will also need an accident book to record any incidents or accidents. (This is essential in the event of any insurance claim. A record of the matter should be noted, along with details of action taken. It should be countersigned where appropriate.)

Technical manager

The amount of technology used will vary with the size and nature of each club but these days it is hard to manage without some technical equipment. A technical manager could take responsibility for:

- Visual – laptop and projector, or OHP; screen, or DVD and TV.
- Audio – PA for presenters and band, CD/MP3 player.

OPTIONAL EXTRAS

Printing and publicity person/team

A computer-literate person, or team of people should take responsibility for all the design, printing and publicity for **Mega Makers!** Your aim should be to produce publicity that is visually impressive, consistent, accurate and attractive.

The publicity will need to be colourful, and use the **Mega Makers!** logo (available on the DVD or website), an attractive, child-friendly font,

PHASE 3

pictures and clip art. The publicity team could take responsibility for:

- Posters and fliers to advertise **Mega Makers!**
- Registration forms for the children to fill in (see sample version on the website).
- Consent forms for parents/guardians/carers (see sample version on the website).
- Invitation cards or letters to go with the appropriate forms.
- Forms for potential team members, including an indication of roles they'd like to take on. You should also send CRB forms out with these forms if the team member has not already had clearance.
- Notes and training materials for the team. Even if someone else writes this material, the printing and publicity team should be responsible for the layout.
- Name badges for the team members and for any adults who are on site and part of **Mega Makers!**
- Signs and notices. These will be needed around the site, including the main hall, entrances, toilets and areas that are out of bounds. These should use the same typeface and colours as other materials to maintain the consistent **Mega Makers!** scheme.
- Prayer cards/bookmarks – prayer pointers to help church members to pray for the holiday club before, during and after **Mega Makers!**

Security, health and safety person

The person in charge of security will be responsible for ensuring that no child leaves the building unless they have permission to do so, and that only children or adults who are part of **Mega Makers!** are allowed to enter the building or area set aside for the club.

It is important for each team member to have an appropriate, clearly labelled badge to identify them and their role. The children registered for **Mega Makers!** should each have their own badge which should be taken off before they leave the club. Any adult or child on site not wearing an appropriate badge should be challenged. Alternatively, each team member and child can be given a new sticky-backed badge each day. Some parents do not like their children to wear pin badges since they can be sharp and can damage clothes.

This person also needs to plan how you will evacuate the building in the event of a fire. Check that fire escapes are kept clear, that the team know the position of fire extinguishers and know what

the fire alarm – or noise that means 'leave the building immediately' – sounds like. Each Engineer should be a roll-call marshal for their Toolshed. The health and safety person is in charge of clearing the building and dealing with the emergency services, but they should allocate responsibility for checking other areas of the building (toilets, snack bar etc) to other team members who will be present each day. You may want to incorporate a fire drill into your programme early in the week. The children will be used to this from school, but it might help the adults!

They should also make sure all the activities are adequately risk-assessed before the club starts.

Registration person/team

Responsible for:

- Allocation of children to Toolsheds.
- Checking children in and out each day.
- Checking forms are completed fully.
- Keeping a check on team sizes if more children register during **Mega Makers!**
- Ensuring each child is to be picked up or has permission to walk home themselves. If you have a lot of children attending the club, it can be hard to keep track of who has permission to collect which child, especially when parents help each other out. A collection slip, which can be given to the adult who will pick the child up, is on the **Mega Makers!** website.

If possible encourage parents of children to complete booking forms in advance to be returned to the leader of the holiday club, school office or community group leader. This means you can allocate children to groups in advance and will inform you of dietary requirements, medical issues and physical, educational or behavioural special needs. Remember to check these when planning the club activities! A register should be made, based on the names and ages provided. A copy of a register must also be given to each Toolshed leader in case of a fire or emergency.

In some contexts, pre-registering is not practical, therefore ensure on the first day that there are plenty of volunteers available to help greet the children and their parents or carers and to provide them with the registration form to fill in. Children should not attend the event if permission has not been granted. As this can be a lengthy process, you should open the doors earlier on Day 1 and during registration, engage the children in parachute games, up-front games or a short film.

The Storyteller

One person or several people could be the storyteller (and it could be Boffin). As such, they must be a confident and skilled communicator. They need to prepare the story thoroughly and be happy telling it to a group of children. Visual aids, props and different methods of storytelling are suggested, some of which will also be of help to the Toolshed leaders in the Bible discovery time. If you are only using the DVD to tell the story, you won't need this role.

Additional up-front roles

Depending on how much Boffin does, you may need to appoint people to explain the Learn and remember verse, interview a team member and lead the activity on praying for the world.

Elastic Eureka

If you have enough leaders, allocate one of them to be Elastic Eureka who ensures that the stretch invention happens each session. Elastic Eureka needs to introduce the stretch invention and prepare team members and children to demonstrate their stretch for children to copy. A stretch invention jingle can be played while the children hold their stretches. If you are short on leaders, Boffin could take on this role.

Assistant Engineers

The role of the assistant is to support the Engineer and ideally should also be available every day. This is a good way to develop the leadership skill of young or inexperienced team members.

All team members should be given training in dealing with children, especially in relation to physical contact and not being with children alone out of sight of others, but Engineers and assistants especially need to be aware of child protection issues and policies.

If you have a large holiday club, you may appoint someone to coordinate six or eight Toolsheds who are all in one age range. It is best if these coordinators do not have a group of their own.

Drama team

The drama involves seven characters and the drama team need to be reasonably confident as actors with the ability to project their voices. The team should be willing to learn their lines and to practise each sketch until they can perform it with confidence. One of the drama team (or another person) needs to take the responsibility of Props Manager, and collect and prepare all the props.

Innovation (the worship band)

Having a live band can add something special to a holiday club. If you can't use live music, then sing along to a CD. The band could be creatively dressed as inventors. If you don't have a live band, you could have a group of dancers instead who lead everyone in actions to songs, either with existing actions or their own.

Construction coordinator

Someone should take responsibility for ensuring all the equipment needed for the construction, creative prayer and Toolshed activities is in the correct place at the right time. Get as much as possible of the craft prepared in advance; there may well be church members who, while they can't help at the club itself, will be happy to help with cutting out etc.

Try to prepare a finished version of each item to show the children what they are making and provide everything needed for each team's resource box (pens, paper, modelling clay etc). Each day this person should explain how the craft is made and supervise the activity.

Games coordinator

This person needs to take responsibility for ensuring all the games equipment is in the correct place at the right time. Each day the games coordinator will need to explain how to play the game and supervise the activity.

TRAINING THE TEAM

However experienced your team, there are two key areas to cover in training: good practice in working with children and delivering the **Mega Makers!** programme itself. Here is a suggested programme for two training sessions: session 2 includes the choice to use the activities outlined in the book or the training feature on the DVD. If possible, aim to use the material from both sessions, but if you don't have time for this, choose the session most appropriate for your team.

Session 1
- **Practicalities**: Basic outline of **Mega Makers!**, learning the theme song, daily structure etc.
- **Skills**: Praying with children
- **Skills**: Reading the Bible with children
- **Skills**: Helping children respond to Jesus
- **Prayer**: For **Mega Makers!** and all who come

Session 2
- **Skills**: Leading small groups (from book or DVD)
- **Practicalities**: Getting the best from the DVD training feature

PHASE 3

SESSION 1

The Mega Makers! programme and working with children

Use this session to go through some of the practical aspects of the club, to help your team understand what will be expected of them and to begin to consider the children who will come to **Mega Makers!**

Welcome

Make sure you give the team a big welcome, ensuring refreshments are freely available, with the **Mega Makers!** theme song playing in the background as people arrive.

Practicalities

Explain the overall themes of **Mega Makers!** (see page 6 and summary sheet on the website). Give an overview of the different roles that people will have. Introduce the team to the Learn and remember verses (see pages 10 and 11), the **Mega Makers!** theme song, Boffin and Brainwave and the other recurring elements of the programme.

Take the team through a day's programme, making sure that everyone knows where all the different parts will take place and their responsibilities in each one.

The aims of Mega Makers!

Make sure everyone has a copy of the general aims of **Mega Makers!** (see page 6) and the specific aims for your club. Split into smaller groups to discuss these aims – can the groups identify any other aims? This will help you refine your aims and encourage your team to take ownership of them.

Legal requirements

Cover health and safety, risk assessments, fire procedures and basic child protection (go to www.scriptureunion.org.uk/holidayclubs for more information). If your church has a coordinator for this, they should be able to help out at this point. Alternatively, contact CCPAS (The Churches' Child Protection Advisory Service) or visit their website: www.ccpas.co.uk

Praying with children

There will be many chances to pray with children during **Mega Makers!** There are two different aspects that come up during **Mega Makers!**: praying about things with children and helping children make a response.

Praying with children

- Ask the children to name some of the things they want to pray for.

- Break these down into things they want to say sorry for, things they want to say thank you to God for, and things they want to ask for themselves or others.
- If you are going to lead the prayer yourself, make sure that you keep to the point and include the suggestions the children made.
- Encourage the children, where possible, to lead the prayers with you.
- Be imaginative in using different ways to pray, eg using pictures or objects to stimulate thought; music to help praise or reflection; prayers with a set response; taking it in turns using one sentence; or prayers using different bodily postures. Suggestions are given each day for praying creatively.
- Take care to use simple, clear modern English, free from jargon, keeping it brief and relevant.

Talking with God should be very natural and the children need to realise this. Explain that we say 'Amen' as a means of saying we agree. We don't have to close our eyes and put our hands together!

 For more information on praying with children, check out *Top Tips on Prompting prayer* (Scripture Union 978 1 84427 322 5 £3.50).

Reading the Bible with children

At **Mega Makers!** we want children to understand that the Bible is God's Word for them today. It is important that the times when you read the Bible together are enjoyable and make sense to them! Children are not simply reading the Bible to get answers to our questions. Instead, we want their curiosity raised so that they can expect to meet God as they read the Bible, not just now, but in the future.

Encourage your team to look at the Bible through the eyes of a child whenever they read it. What would a child find hard? What would they enjoy? What would they be most likely to remember from the passage? Just as children see the world at a different physical level, they often see spiritual things differently too, so encourage everyone to think from a child's perspective.

Helping children to respond

Much of the material you will cover in **Mega Makers!** may prompt children to want to be friends with God or Jesus for themselves. Be ready to help them, but make sure that you stay within your church's child protection policy when praying with children.

- Unless you bring up the subject, a child may not have the words to begin a conversation about responding to Jesus. Explain that if at any time they do want to talk to you more, they should say 'Tell me more about Jesus', and then you will know what they want to discuss.
- They rarely need long explanations, just simple answers to questions.
- Talk to them in a place where you can be seen by others.
- Never put pressure on children to respond in a particular way, just help them take one step closer to Jesus when they are ready. We don't want them to respond just to please us!
- Treat each as an individual. So don't say, 'Hands up who wants to follow Jesus?' or make children say something that is not true for them, but allow each one to choose what is right for them.
- Always allow children a way out: give them an opportunity to go away and think about their decision and come back to you either later in the session or on the following day. This is God's work, and even if you don't have the chance to talk to them again he can actually achieve it without you!
- Remember, many children move through a number of stages of commitment to Jesus as their understanding grows.
- Many children just need a bit of help to say what they want to say to God. Here is a suggested prayer they could use to express their belief in Jesus and desire to belong to him:

Jesus, I want to become a follower of Jesus.
Thank you that you love me.
Thank you for living in the world and dying
    on a cross for me.
I'm sorry for all the wrong things I have
    done.
Please forgive me so that I might become
    your follower.
Please let the Holy Spirit help me be like
    you.
Amen.

- Reassure them that God hears us when we talk with him and has promised to forgive us and help us to be his friends. Children need help to stick with Jesus, especially if their parents and/or others around them don't believe.

- Assure them that God wants to hear whatever they say. Give them some prayer ideas.
- Encourage them to keep coming to Christian activities, not necessarily on Sundays – their church might have to be the midweek club or a school lunch-time club.
- Reading the Bible will be easier with something like *Snapshots through the Year* or *Snapshots 365* – but you need to support them if they are to keep it up.
- Keep praying and maintain your relationship with them wherever possible.

Friends with Jesus (for 5 to 7s), *Me+Jesus* (for 8s and 9s) and *Jesus=friendship forever* will help to explain what it means to follow Jesus. Details are on the inside front cover.

 For more information on helping children respond, see *Top Tips on Helping a child respond to Jesus* (Scripture Union 978 1 84427 387 4 £2.99).

Prayer

End your session with prayer for **Mega Makers!** Draw a large 'gingerbread' child on a sheet of paper; give out sticky notes and pens to everyone and invite them to write prayers on them that are about asking God to help you deal with the specific situations you have considered in this session: the programme, reading the Bible, praying with children and helping children to respond. Then invite everyone to come in turn and stick their prayers on the shape, and to pray briefly either silently or aloud for those things.

SESSION 2

Leading a small group

Leading a small group of children is a vital part of **Mega Makers!** Engineers and assistants will be the ones who get to know and build relationships with the children, in their Toolsheds. Sometimes these relationships can develop into long-term friendships. Understanding how these groups work and having a set of guidelines are really important. There is an excellent training feature on leading small groups available on the **Mega Makers!** DVD which you can watch together, followed by discussion. Alternatively use the following to stimulate thinking about leading a small group.

Small-group role play

If you have a fairly confident group of leaders, try this role-play activity. Six or seven leaders play

PHASE 3

typical children in a group, and one person is the Toolshed leader. This small group is going to look at the *Inventor's Sheets* activity from Day 1 (see page 83). Split your team into groups of seven or eight, and make sure you provide enough sets of the character descriptions (see below) and everything that you need for the *Inventor's Sheets* activity.

Give out the character descriptions and tell the teams not to show anyone their piece of paper, but to act it out during the activity as best they can. Encourage the team not to overact and make their group leader's role a total nightmare, but to take it as seriously as they can.

- You are the Toolshed leader. Your group has lots of needs, and you should try very hard to include everyone in the discussion and keep the discussion on track!
- You are an intelligent child who knows all the answers and keeps putting their hand up to answer, or to ask a question, but you don't call out or interrupt.
- You are a very shy younger child, who will be very slow in interacting with the group.
- You are a fidgeter who can't keep still, yet is following what is being discussed.
- You are a child who naturally interrupts all the time, but should respond to firm handling by your Engineer. You should ask to go to the toilet at least once during the short group time.
- You are an average sort of child, who is interested in the teaching and discussion. You have got a bit of a crush on your leader, so go and sit next to them if you can and maintain eye contact.
- You listen well and follow all that your leader asks you to do, making a valuable contribution to the group.
- You are deeply committed to Jesus and yet find it very difficult to articulate how you feel or what to say. You try very hard to contribute to the group.

Feedback from the role play

The activity should be a good, fun way of raising some of the issues involved in leading a small group. Have some flip-chart paper and markers ready to note down any interesting points to come from the groups.

Talk first to the Toolshed leader, encouraging them that at **Mega Makers!** it will never be as difficult as the last few minutes! Ask them to outline the characters in their group. What was difficult to deal with? Who contributed? Who didn't contribute and why?

Discuss some of the issues raised by the characters, eg What are you going to do about the child who always asks to go to the toilet? How should you handle leader crushes?

By the time the feedback has finished you should have a set of guidelines for leading a group. Below are a few dos and don'ts which may be worth adding to discussion at the end.

Dos and don'ts of leading a small group

- Do learn their names and call them by name.
- Do take notice of how each child behaves, reacts and interacts so you can get to know each one quickly.
- Do take the initiative. Let them know clearly what you expect from the group, how each one is valued and encouraged to participate in the life of the group.
- Do be specific in your prompting and questions (this can help everyone contribute).
- Do try to meet the children's needs (each child will come with their own needs).
- Don't assume that all the children will learn from or experience the club in the same way.
- Do be polite and patient (even if one or two children really annoy you!).
- Do add oodles of enthusiasm to your group (they will pick up on your attitude – you are a role model).
- Do think creatively, eg how you sit, lie or kneel as a group to discuss things. One way would be for everyone in the group (including leaders) to lie on the floor on their tummies in a circle with heads in to the centre.
- Do model what you expect the children to do, eg responding with enthusiasm to the drama!
- Do be careful to follow closely any instructions or notes you are given.
- Do ask for help if you need it (you are not alone!).
- Do be careful with language (no jargon, complicated or inappropriate language).
- Do pray for them and yourself as you lead the group.
- Don't make favourites.
- Do not be physical with them (this can be misinterpreted).

Here are a few extra thoughts about keeping control to guide you

The key to establishing good discipline and control is relationship-building and clear expectations –

these need to be thought through before **Mega Makers!** starts. This can be done by:

- Setting some ground rules and boundaries for the group – and sticking to them!
- Having plenty of materials for everyone.
- Ensuring you are fully prepared with everything you need to hand. Failure in this can open the door for behaviour problems!
- Ensuring that you have enough leaders at all times.
- Positively reinforcing the children's behaviour when they answer or do something well.
- Never sacrificing the needs of the group for one child.

 For more information on leading small groups, check out *Top Tips on Leading small groups* (Scripture Union 978 1 84427 388 1 £2.99).

 For more information on managing behaviour, see *Mega Top Tips: Dealing with Challenging Behaviour* (Scripture Union 978 1 84427 531 1 £4.99).

Other useful information for your team

Working with special or additional needs

During **Mega Makers!** you will face a number of challenges. Being prepared to take care of children with special or additional needs can be a tremendous blessing to both the children and their parent or carers. Photocopy the guidelines on page 93 for working with children with additional needs.

 Top Tips on Welcoming special children Scripture Union 978 1 84427 126 9 £3.50 Helping children with special needs to know God is challenging, but deeply rewarding. Find out what the Bible has to say on the subject and explore the implications of the Disability Discrimination Act for your church. Be encouraged and inspired with stories from group leaders and parents, and be equipped with lots of practical ideas for welcoming special children in your church and children's group.

Working with children from other faith backgrounds

Having children from different faiths come to our events is a great privilege. Knowing that their parents trust us to care for their children and are willing to allow us to share the Good News of Jesus is exciting, but also gives us a responsibility to think about how we are going to treat the children

and relate to their faith and culture. The principles on page 93 have been worked out by practitioners with many years' experience of working in this context. Whilst you might not agree with all of them we think they are worth serious consideration in order to ensure that we give a genuine welcome to children from other faith backgrounds. We have written these recognizing that whilst some parents from different faiths are keen for their children to attend a club run by Christians they might still have strong objections to their children becoming followers of Jesus. It is with this and other tensions in mind that we have produced a page of principles which can be photocopied and given to Engineers, if you expect to have children from other faith backgrounds attending. In addition it is worth reminding your team of the importance of treating the Bible as a holy book: never simply put it down on the floor, but always place it carefully on a table (and especially don't use it to raise the height of a projector, for example!) Be sure that you use copies that are in good condition, as one which is falling apart would be shameful to some children from other faith backgrounds. If you are serving food at any activities, check that it will be appropriate for any child from another faith background.

 Top Tips on Welcoming children of other faiths Scripture Union 978 1 84427 250 1 £3.50 What does the Bible say about those of other faiths and how we should live out our faith amongst them? What can your church do? Here's a readable and practical guide which will inspire and equip you to build relationships with children and their families. It's packed with practical, fun ideas that will strengthen or even kick-start your ministry with those of other faiths.

 Top Tips on Communicating God in non-book ways (Scripture Union 978 1 84427 329 4 £3.50)

 Top Tips on Discovering the Bible with children (Scripture Union 978 1 84427 335 5 £3.50)

 Top Tips: Running Holiday Clubs (Scripture Union 978 1 84427 541 0 £3.50)

PHASE 3

All in a day's work

PLANNING YOUR SESSION

When you come to plan each day, make sure you have read the descriptions of the programme in Phase 1. Select the activities according to the children you are likely to have at the club. You do not need to include all the activities listed here in your programme.

MAKING YOUR CHOICE

There are many factors which will influence your choice of activities:

The children involved

The children should be the most important consideration when choosing the daily activities. Children respond differently to the same activity. Engineers in particular should bear this in mind when planning Power drill.

The length of the club

Simply, if you have a long club, then you will be able to do more! The timings given are merely guidelines; different children will take different lengths of time to complete the same activity. Be flexible in your timings, judge whether it would be more valuable to complete an activity, even though it may be overrunning, rather than cut it short and go on to the next activity. Have something in your programme you can drop if things overrun.

The leaders available

Not every club will be able to find leaders with the necessary skills to fulfil every requirement. If you can't find anyone with a Basic Food Hygiene Certificate, you will have to limit the refreshments you can provide. If you don't have musicians, then you'll have to rely on backing tracks or miss out the singing.

To help Engineers prepare for Power drill, the questions for each day are called 'Bible discovery' and can be found in the relevant section for that day and on the **Mega Makers!** website.

SUNDAY 1 THE MESSAGE OF JESUS

Louder & louder

Key passage
Matthew 3:1–17; 4:17

Key storylines
⊙ John the Baptist bursts onto the scene, calling people to turn back to God.
⊙ John baptises Jesus in the River Jordan.
⊙ Jesus himself begins to preach the same message with the invitation to turn back to God.

Key aims
⊙ To hear how John the Baptist came to announce that Jesus had come and how people needed to listen to his life-changing message.
⊙ To launch the holiday club so that church members can commit to pray for the coming week.
⊙ To welcome any children and parents/carers coming to the club who are not usually part of the worshipping community.

For children and their families with no church background
Children and adults will be present in church for a variety of reasons. Adults may have come to accompany the children but have little interest in the Christian faith. On the other hand, they themselves may be searching for God and registering their child for **Mega Makers!** may be part of their faith journey. The children will also have mixed experiences of church and understanding of the Christian faith. Each of them needs to be welcomed and helped to enjoy the service. Think about what will be unfamiliar to them, for example when to stand and when to sit, and what words they may not understand. It's good to involve in the service in some way the people they know, at least in planning it, preferably in presenting it.

For church children
Encourage church children to look out for their friends who don't usually come and sit with them to help them feel part of what is going on. Some church children take part in the service. By involving them you can help them feel part of the holiday club in a special way.

For children and their families from other faiths
If you do have children and their families coming to this first service make sure they receive a genuine but not overwhelming welcome. It may be their first visit to a church so have someone on hand to explain what is happening throughout the service and to reassure them that it's OK just to watch and listen rather than join in the singing or prayers. At the end, introduce them to other children and families with whom they could form friendships. If they are coming to a church service they will expect it to be a Christian act of worship so there is no need to 'water down' the message.

For children with additional needs
Parents will value your non-judgemental acceptance of their child. Ask parents or carers how best to welcome their child since they need to be confident that their child will be included, encouraged and kept safe. As you begin to make friends with the child, assume that they are able to understand you. Just because a child cannot speak, move or see does not mean that they do not understand. Each child will want to be treated the same as any other child of the same age.

PHASE 4

Service outline

What-you-need checklist
You will need:

- [ ] Someone from the drama team dressed up as John the Baptist
- [ ] Messages for the introductory activity
- [ ] Copies of the Bible reading and three readers
- [ ] A flip chart and pens
- [ ] An artist able to draw three simple sets of faces.

Suggested songs
Songs should be about God's love and his ever-expanding greatness. They can be confessional since this is a service of Christian worship but be aware that visitors may not know the songs and may not want to sing words that they neither understand nor believe.

- ⊙ Come on and celebrate *The Source* 75
- ⊙ Come, now is the time to worship *Songs of Fellowship* 1205
- ⊙ Our God is an awesome God *The Source* 418
- ⊙ Our God is a great big God *Songs of Fellowship* 2004
- ⊙ Make way, make way *The Source* 349
- ⊙ God's love is deeper *kidsource* 84
- ⊙ Great is thy faithfulness *The Source* 138
- ⊙ **Mega Makers!** theme song See pages 88 to 90

Welcome
Welcome everyone and explain that the service may be a little different from your usual style, as it is the launch of **Mega Makers!** Talk briefly about the holiday club so everyone is aware of what is happening in the week ahead. The club's theme and the role of the Mega Machine will become clearer through the service. (You will need to decide how much you want to share in advance about the Mega Machine and other aspects of the club and whether you want to introduce Boffin and Brainwave. You might also like to introduce the drama and get the drama team to perform the short sketch available for today (see script on page 76).

Start with a song(s) that recognises that we are welcomed into God's presence as we come to worship – see above for suggestions.

Set the scene
Someone dressed as John the Baptist storms down the aisle or towards the front, speaking quietly and gets louder and louder as he gets to the front, 'Make way! Make way! Get ready! Change your hearts and minds because the kingdom of heaven is near!' The service leader then asks 'John the Baptist' who he is and why he has interrupted the service. He answers saying that he has an important message from God for everyone to hear – when John the Baptist lived (2,000 years ago) and now! (This is why he ended up shouting out so loudly in the service.) Then explain that in the service you will be hearing more about John the Baptist and what it was that he was (and is) shouting about louder and louder.

Acknowledge that sometimes we do not listen to what God is saying to us. Use the prayer below, inviting people to respond with the **emboldened** words.

Leader: Father God, John wanted people to get ready because the kingdom of heaven was near! That was why he shouted with such urgency.

All: Help us to listen and obey.

Leader: Father God, you call us to pay attention to what you say.

All: Help us to listen and obey.

Leader: Father God, forgive us for the times this week when we have failed to live as people who know your love, and we have shut you out of our lives.

All: Help us to listen and obey.

Leader: This week we pray that everyone taking part in holiday club will listen to what you are saying to them.

All: Help us all to listen and obey.

Introductory activity
Explain that in **Mega Makers!** the children will be witnessing the launch of the Mega Machine which enlarges everything that goes into it. It has been developed by our two inventors, Boffin and Brainwave. The Machine could be on view and you might even demonstrate how it works. Or you may wish to delay its official launch until the start of the club. Throughout the club everyone will discover that God's love gets greater and greater, wider and wider, deeper and deeper and goes on for ever and ever. That is why you have heard John the Baptist calling out his message louder and louder.

Since a voice getting louder and louder is part of this service's theme it would be a good idea to play a loud/soft voice game. This 'game' could be a version of Chinese whispers where one message is whispered by one person to several others standing in a line. How far has the 'message' been distorted by the time it gets to the end of the line? The message could be 'Prepare the way for the Lord', or 'Make the road straight for the Lord.'

Bible reading
The following is taken from the Contemporary English Version (which is the version we are using in **Mega Makers!**) of Matthew 3:1–8,11,13–16; 4:17. You will need three people (who have practised beforehand) as readers. The main reader/narrator reads with a normal reading voice, depending upon the effectiveness of the PA, and readers 2 and 3 join in to add volume at the appropriate places.

Narrator: [1] Years later, John the Baptist started preaching in the desert of Judea. [2] He said, 'Turn back to God! The kingdom of heaven will soon be here.' [3] John was the one the prophet Isaiah was talking about, when he said:

Narrator plus **Reader 2** *getting louder as they read*: 'In the desert someone is shouting

Narrator plus **Readers 2** and **3** *shouting out*: "Get the road ready for the Lord! Make a straight path for him."'

Narrator: [4] John wore clothes made of camel's hair. He had a leather strap around his waist and ate grasshoppers and wild honey.
[5] From Jerusalem and all Judea and from the Jordan River Valley crowds of

people went to John. [6] They told how sorry they were for their sins, and he baptised them in the river.

[7] Many Pharisees and Sadducees also came to be baptised. But John said to them: 'You bunch of snakes! Who warned you to run from the coming judgment? [8] Do something to show that you have really given up your sins.'

Narrator *reads getting louder*: John announced: [11] 'I baptise you with water so that you will give up your sins.

Narrator and **Reader 1** *read getting louder*: But someone more powerful is going to come, and I am not good enough even to carry his sandals.

Narrator *plus* **Readers 1** *and* **2**: He will baptise you with the Holy Spirit and with fire.

Narrator: [13] Jesus left Galilee and went to the Jordan River to be baptised by John. [14] But John kept objecting and said, 'I ought to be baptised by you. Why have you come to me?'

[15] Jesus answered, 'For now this is how it should be, because we must do all that God wants us to do.' Then John agreed.

[16] So Jesus was baptised. And as soon as he came out of the water, the sky opened, and he saw the Spirit of God coming down on him like a dove. [17] Then a voice from heaven said, 'This is my own dear Son, and I am pleased with him.'

Narrator *plus* **Readers 1** *and* **2** *as loud as they can*: [4:17] Then Jesus started preaching, 'Turn back to God! The kingdom of heaven will soon be here.'

Bible talk

Storytelling method: drawing

Lots of different people came to hear John the Baptist shouting out his message in the desert. He really, really believed that what he had to say was the most important message anyone could ever hear. He was calling people back to God saying that someone far greater than him was coming who would judge all people. But there would be a difference between

those who had turned back to God and those who had not, those who wanted to change their hearts and lives and those who did not. This person would bring God into people's lives. We know that this person was God himself, Jesus.

Jesus then came and was baptised with water. God the Father in heaven spoke saying, 'This is my Son and I am pleased with him!' The Spirit of God came down from the sky like a dove and rested on Jesus. Wow!

Explore the different ways people reacted to John the Baptist's message.

The crowds *'Artist' to draw lots of simple faces together as though in crowd, either with mouths wide open or mouths smiling. They could also draw some droplets of water on the faces of the crowd when you talk about them being baptised, although it almost certainly was not baptism by sprinkling!*

The crowds had hurried into the desert to hear John's message. Many of them were curious to hear John's message and listened open-mouthed. Some of them, though, were convinced by John's challenge to turn back to God and realised that living in a way that does not please God was wrong. They wanted to be baptised as a sign of wanting to 'give up their sins' that is, live to please God, which was by far the best way to live. The water was a sign that they were being made clean from their wrongdoing.

The Pharisees and Sadducees *Artist to draw a few faces with downturned mouths –men only*

The Pharisees and Sadducees were religious leaders and they were very critical of anyone who said things that they disagreed with. They came to hear John's message and Matthew even says that they wanted to be baptised. But John knew that in their hearts they did not want to 'give up their sins' or take his message seriously. In fact, they criticised Jesus' message even more and three years later they put him to death. John knew that God could see what they really thought.

Jesus *Artist to draw one face only, head*

bowed, mouth one straight line, with a dove dropping onto his head and droplets of water on his face.

When Jesus arrived (he was in fact John's cousin) John knew straightaway that this was the one he had been speaking about. Jesus wanted to be baptised and insisted that John should do it. (John did not think he was good enough.) As Jesus came up out of the water in the River Jordan, God the Father spoke and affirmed the fact that Jesus really was this promised one, his Son. Jesus then began his job of travelling round telling people about God, healing people and performing some amazing miracles. He began by preaching exactly the same message as John (see 3:2 and 4:17) and spent three years making it clearer and clearer what John meant – we could say that Jesus was shouting out his message louder and louder.

So how do we respond to this message from God?

Go through the options of being curious, of being critical and thinking this is all wrong, or actually of wanting to turn back to God, trusting that John's and Jesus' message is true. We too need to follow Jesus.

Explain that this is what the central theme and message of **Mega Makers!** is. Children will hear how Jesus invited people to follow him, to become like him and to change their hearts and lives. (Give more details of how the club is going to run.)

Prayer

Lead several short prayers about the things that people will be doing this week. Children and team members could take part in this. Pray for the leaders, for the children, for all the practical details and safety, and give thanks to God that everyone has the opportunity to hear Jesus' message.

DAY 1 THE INVITATION TO FOLLOW JESUS

Wider & wider

Key passage
Matthew 9:9–13

Key storylines
- Jesus invited Matthew to follow him. Matthew was a tax collector, despised by many people who saw him as someone who collaborated with the Roman authorities and was probably a cheat!
- Matthew later invited Jesus to have dinner with him and his friends and acquaintances. This meant that Jesus met some of the unsavoury characters Matthew associated with.
- The Machine 'receives' small bread rolls and spits out huge loaves of bread.
- Storytelling method: Children call out 'Boo' and 'Hurray' at appropriate times and lots of invitation cards are needed.

Key aims
- To welcome each child to the club, setting the tone for the next few days.
- To help children grasp that Jesus' invitation started with a few people but was spread wider and wider, to all sorts of people, of all ages and included those who were popular.
- To plant the truth from the start that Jesus invites everyone at **Mega Makers!** to follow him, whatever they are like, whatever their background. His invitation is offered to a wider and wider group of people.
- To enable children to see the vastness of God's love for them.

For children with no church background

The story of Jesus calling fishermen to become his followers is sometimes told in RE lessons for KS1 (infants) children but the call of Matthew is less familiar. All children need to grasp the background to this story. If they have travelled abroad they might know the phrase 'duty free', and will almost certainly have passed through the 'NOTHING TO DECLARE' channel in customs. The payment of a tax to transport goods (which was Matthew's business) may make sense to some.

The second part of the story is about a meal with Jesus which is of interest to anyone who likes food. Children may be puzzled by the term 'sinner' which is commonly used today with no reference to God but just means being a bit naughty. Jesus explained that he came not for good people but for sinners. We would define a 'sinner' in this context as people who don't live the way God wants them to.

For church children

Little is known about Matthew (also known as Levi) even though he is the named author of this Gospel. Is this because Matthew kept dubious company so Jesus' call to the more appealing fishermen is better known? The message of this story is powerful especially for church children. These days Jesus has certainly come to call people who have grown up in church to follow him. They have had many opportunities to accept his invitation. But he has also come to call those who so far have not heard much about him. Here is the challenge for church children to reach out to those more on the margins of their society (which includes children!). How wonderful it would be if, as part of Mega Makers!, many children would want to share Jesus with their friends and those who are less loved and popular. Jesus' love reaches out to them too.

For children with other faiths

All the major faiths will have an understanding of the 'wrongness' of collaborating with the enemy. Children from many African, South Asian and Semitic/Arab cultures will recognise the importance of eating together – and of who is invited and who accepts the invitation. For Hindu children there may be echoes of the caste system and a parallel to be drawn between accepting an invitation from those of a different caste or even no caste. High caste Hindu children may find this scandalous. Sikh children may be used to the concept of welcoming and feeding whoever arrives for the meal, as this is the way their Gurdwaras (temples) operate.

For children with additional needs

Remember that some children with additional needs will take longer to settle in on the first day because everything is new and strange. Try showing them around the building when they arrive, and make a visual diary using either Makaton-style symbols or photos so they can see what happens when.

Engineers' briefing

Spiritual preparation

Read Matthew 9:9–13

Talk about what might have been going through the minds of the Pharisees and Matthew's friends whom he invited to eat with Jesus. What was it about Jesus that made some people question and judge him while others accepted him?

Comment that Jesus encountered a wide range of people in his ministry. You are likely to have a wide variety of children coming to **Mega Makers!** Ask what differences there will be between the children – eg boys and girls, ages, sizes, family backgrounds, faith backgrounds, from different churches, different schools, on their own or with friends – just as the team of leaders is made up of different people. Jesus invites every one of you to follow him.

In the light of these differences pray for the children who are coming, asking God that each child will feel welcomed.

Practical preparation

Talk through the programme. Remind people of the key learning aims and who is doing what, making sure everyone knows their role and has everything they need. Check that younger team members or those who have not been involved before are OK. Encourage them during the session too. The overall leader could do this or it could be assigned to another member of the team, or member of the church whose sole role is to encourage the team. It is important that people feel able to ask about anything they are not 100 per cent clear about.

Set up the different areas of the club, making sure everything is in place in plenty of time, so you are ready as the first children come from the registration area. You will probably need extra help as it is the first day. Leaders should be especially welcoming to parents and children who have not been before or any adults accompanying children who look uncomfortable being in a church setting.

The concept of 'wider and wider' may be hard to understand for some children. As they settle in, play a fun game with your hands showing the space between them getting wider and wider in different directions. Ask them to play the game by doing it too, or ask them to say the word 'wider' as an instruction to make you move your hands wider apart. You could then use this during Power drill to help them understand.

What-you-need checklist

You will need:

- [ ] **Registration**: registration forms, badges, labels, pens, team lists
- [ ] **The Mega Machine**: the equipment to complete it; two bread rolls and a large round loaf
- [ ] **The Brainbox**: for jokes, messages, questions and pictures
- [ ] **Messy mechanics**: ingredients to make the dough, bowls, flour, aprons, covering for the floor
- [ ] **Technology**: PA system, laptop, PowerPoints and projection/OHP and acetates, **Mega Makers!** DVD
- [ ] **Toolsheds**: material for mini-machines and opening and closing activities; Bibles, *Inventor's Notebooks* or *Inventor's Sheets*
- [ ] **Music**: Innovation band or backing tracks
- [ ] **Drama**: costumes and props
- [ ] **Activities**: equipment for games and construction
- [ ] **Boffin and Brainwave** (presenters): running order, equipment for Mega words, the Learn and remember verse, praying for the wide world, quiz questions
- [ ] **From the Maker's Manual**: story script, two individual invitations in an envelope and a pile of ten invitations stuck together
- [ ] **Down tools**: Drinks and biscuits or other refreshments

Listen to any last-minute information or instructions from Boffin and Brainwave, or from the drama, music or refreshment team.

Programme

Clocking in

10 minutes

As this is the first day of the club, make sure the registration team with extra helpers are ready to greet and register the children so that any new children and

PHASE 4

parents don't have to wait long. Have a welcome team on hand to take the children to their Toolshed.

It is important that children can relate to their Toolshed leaders who will be with them all the time of the club. Relationship-building and trust begins as soon as each child is welcomed into the Toolshed! These first few minutes are vitally important. Leaders should be familiar with the names of expected children and use the name of each child as much as they can. Introduce unknown children to one another and begin to decorate your Toolshed and make a mini-machine unique to your group of children. For ideas of how to do this, see page 17.

Alternatively, introduce the idea of inventions in one of two ways. All gadgets and machines have to be invented by someone! In advance, print off resource page 92 of the list of ten inventors, their invention and its date. Cut these out as shown on the sheet and lay them out on the floor in categories but with each category muddled up. Can the children match them up? As they arrive they can join in with another child or pair to do this together. Getting the dates right will be the real challenge!

Or print off on card a copy of the pictures of the ten inventions from the website, cutting the pictures to make playing cards. Play a simple game of snap with groups of four or five.

Ask children to name other inventions or inventors – or you could suggest some.

The inventor's workshop
45 minutes all together

Once all the children are settled in the workshop, Boffin and Brainwave, the inventor and his apprentice introduce themselves, setting a slapstick tone to the programme. Boffin is a studious-looking type whereas Brainwave is a fuss pot who keeps getting things mixed up and lacks confidence in both Boffin's machine and in his ability to make anything work.

Establish three ground rules which might be:
- what to do if the fire or smoke alarm goes off
- where the toilets are and whether you need to ask before you go
- in any small group time, only one person talks at a time when it is their turn

Stretch inventions

Elastic Eureka calls three leaders to the front having primed them to invent a body position which they can hold in a frozen position for 15 seconds. Two leaders could devise a position together, such as one leader goes down on their right knee, holds the left foot of the other leader, who raises both arms in a triangular shape above the head, while the kneeling leader places their face on their other knee. Each child or pair has to attempt to copy this invented position and then hold it for 15 seconds (or longer if the children are able to sustain it). Play a stretch invention jingle while the children 'stretch'.

On subsequent days, ask older children to devise a body position, but do check that it is physically possible for younger children to imitate. Leaders' bodies may be less flexible than children's!

Mega Machine

Boffin assisted by Brainwave has been creating a Mega Machine and today is the topping off occasion. However your machine has been created (see page 5) you need to leave something incomplete, whether it is a surface that needs painting, a piece of scaffolding or a ladder that needs installing, or a flag to be put in place! Boffin invites children to contribute to this act of completion amidst a fanfare of noise and applause. Now the Machine has to go through a strict series of trials, which will continue throughout the club.

Devise a dramatic way of switching on the Machine, such as pulling down a handle, turning on a light, making a klaxon sound. Build up the sense of suspense. The first trial is set in motion. What will it be? Boffin is puzzled and muddled!

Brainwave loses interest and starts eating his lunch of two bread rolls, but gets told off for making a mess. Boffin then has the bright idea that the first trial will be to deposit Brainwave's other bread roll into the Machine to see what emerges. Despite Brainwave's protest, the roll is deposited into the machine, there are grunts, bangs, steam, water etc and finally out pops... a large loaf of bread! Much applause!

Messy mechanics

Invite two leaders and two children to come to the front and pair off one child to one leader. Each pair needs a mixing bowl, wooden spoon, ingredients needed to make bread dough and simple instructions on how to make it, all laid out on a table. (If you have not made bread dough before, seek advice for the recipe and technique most trusted by your adviser!) Ensure you also have something to cover the floor.

The leader, after looking at the table, is blindfolded and the child gives instructions on how to make the bread dough but can't touch anything. The leader must follow the instructions and find everything; the first to finish wins.

Then talk about how yeast makes dough enlarge over time. **Mega Makers!** is all about things getting bigger and bigger! When the children come back to the workshop after Power drill they can see how much the dough has risen. Roll all the dough into one large lump, placing it in a large container, marking how far up the side the dough is, so that it is obvious how much it has risen. Cover with a cloth and leave in a warm place. (It might be a good idea to have a stand by – 'here's one I made earlier' – in case the above doesn't work!)

Music makers

Introduce Innovation, the band (if you have one) and get them to teach the **Mega Makers!** theme song and any actions, if you've come up with some. Sing it a couple of times so that the Mechanics begin to get the hang of it, rather than singing other songs at this point. Say that you'll sing it again later!

From the Maker's Manual

Boffin declares how glad he is that so many children have come to the launch of The Machine. Everyone is welcome. But he has heard that some people never got their invitation to come to view it, some people just didn't want to come and some people didn't want to come because they had heard that Brainwave was going to be there! How shocking is that! And that reminds him of a story which our storyteller (name) is going to share with you all.

Storytelling options

Each day, there are three options suggested for telling the Bible story: you can use the same approach each time, mix and match how you tell the story, or combine two or more approaches. Choose which will be most helpful for your team, your children and the style of your club.

- ◉ The storyteller tells the story based on Matthew 9:9–13 using their own words if possible. You can use the section headings and interactive ideas from the script (see option 3) as memory joggers and to vary your story presentation each time.
- ◉ Introduce today's episode from the **Mega Makers!** DVD. (If you are telling the story and using the DVD, tell the story first, then show the DVD so the children already have the outline of the events before seeing the episode.) In today's episode Bob and Gemma will be at the Eden Project in Cornwall, exploring their incredible 'biomes' made of hexagonal sections that lock together and form the perfect environment for a riot of awesome plant life that couldn't otherwise exist in the UK. This in turn will lead us into Bob telling us about the calling of Matthew, and how Jesus invites everyone to be his friends. Just like the 'biomes', God's love is wide enough to include us all!
- ◉ Or the storyteller may prefer to follow the fully scripted retold Bible story for Day 1 on pages 70 and 71.

Storytelling method: child participation and props.
The storyteller needs to make sure they are familiar with the script so that they can tell the story fluently, preferably in their own words, maintaining eye contact with the children. The storyteller is dressed in casual clothes but with something smart to put on to go to a party, such as a scarf, fascinator or bow tie. The storyteller should have a leader to hold up signs to indicate when the children shout 'Boo' or 'Hurray!'

You will also need the three kinds of invitations which can be downloaded from the **Mega Makers!** website:

- ◉ a large invitation from Matthew to Jesus in an envelope, labelled 'Jesus of Nazareth'
- ◉ a large invitation from Jesus to Matthew in an envelope, labelled 'Matthew, the tax collector'
- ◉ a set of at least 10 A4 sheets with 10 invitations from Jesus to others printed on each which are stuck together as a long strip, ideally perforated, to be torn and separated easily.

Mega words

Each day has a key phrase (which is in two parts: the 'expanding words', and the subject of expansion). This will help children to remember what they have learnt and will keep leaders focused on the message they want children to learn. Jumble up the words of today's phrase and write them on a long/wide strip of paper - similar to the long strip of invitations above. Ask two children to cut up the words, give one word each to eight younger children and then arrange the words in the right order. Today's phrase is:

'**WIDER AND WIDER** - the invitation to follow Jesus'

Ask an engineer

Boffin asks a leader (who is not going to be embarrassed) if he can measure how wide their leg span is if they stretch their legs out wide, almost as far as they can. A couple of children can help. Then ask if they can get their stretch wider and wider. Measure again (with a bit of huffing and puffing) and the stretch has increased.

Ask the leader how many people they know who have heard and accepted Jesus' invitation to follow him. Boffin comments on how wide Jesus' invitation has gone, then asks if more people are hearing and wanting to follow Jesus (with the answer, Yes!). Why do they think Jesus' invitation is so wide and gets wider and wider to include everyone? (Because this is how wide God's love is.) This naturally leads on to the Learn and remember verse.

Ask how they know that they are a follower of Jesus.

Learn and remember

'I pray that you, together with all God's people, may have the power to understand how broad and long, how high and deep, is Christ's love.'

Ephesians 3:18 (GNB)

This verse helps children grasp that Jesus' love is far beyond what any of us can understand but God gives us the power to begin to grasp and experience God with us. This is central to the theme of **Mega Makers!**

Explain that the apostle Paul spent a lot of time in a city on the western coast of Turkey, called Ephesus, where he told others about Jesus. Later he wrote a letter to the people who lived there, who had accepted the invitation to follow Jesus. Here are some of the things he wrote to them which we can read in the Bible in his letter to the Ephesians, chapter 3 verse 18. Use the following signs to help them to remember.

Paul wanted them to know how wide Jesus' love was (*open arms out wide in a semi-circle*), how long Jesus' love was (*stretch your arms out as far as you can*), how high Jesus' love was (*stretch up as high as you can*) and how deep Jesus' love was (*stretch down as low as you can*). Display the words of verse 18 and repeat it several times with actions.

Use the Learn and remember verse song with actions.

PHASE 4.

Power drill
45 minutes in small groups

Down tools
Make sure children are comfortable in their Toolsheds, as they settle for their refreshments. With younger children who can take longer over this, you may want to begin talking about the story as they drink their drinks.

Bible discovery
With older children (8–11s)
Talk about the children's favourite inventions and what they think is particularly good about them. You could name a few of your favourites to get them started. Then turn to page 7 of *Inventor's Notebook* and ask the children to fill in the names of the inventions by using the codecracker on page 4. You might like to take a vote on which of these they rate the highest.

Read Matthew 9 verses 9–13 on pages 8 and 10 of *Inventor's Notebook*. On page 9 get the children to draw where Matthew was sitting and to find the hidden coins. As they do this, talk about whether they think Matthew knew much about Jesus or whether he decided to follow Jesus on impulse. (*Jesus had been around some time performing miracles and teaching, so it is unlikely that Matthew knew nothing about him. Jesus was a local boy from the area around the Lake of Galilee.*)

Invite the children to draw the following people at Matthew's dinner: two guests, one of Jesus' close friends and Jesus, on page 11. Explain that people in those days ate lying down, leaning on their right elbow, with their feet sticking outwards. Talk about the fact that the tax collectors and sinners were not really nice people to have as friends or to go to parties with and ask the children why they think Jesus wanted to mix with this sort of person. (*Jesus cared for people from a very wide selection of society, including lots of outsiders and social misfits.*)

Ask the children if they have ever been to a party or been friends with people who others don't like or look down on. Talk about whether Jesus would have joined their group of friends or come to a party like that.

Invite the children to draw the Pharisee on the grey cross. Explain that the Pharisees were the teachers of the Law of Moses who did not like what Jesus said or did.

Ask the children what they thought Jesus meant when he said he was like a doctor and get them to put their answer in the speech bubble on page 12. You may need to go into some explanation here to help their understanding (There's one on page 13 of *Inventor's Notebook*.) Ask the children if they'd been at Matthew's meal where they would be in the room – sitting with Jesus and Matthew's friends or standing in the corner with the Pharisee.

With younger children (5–8s)
Ask the children to think about if they were having some friends around to play or eat with them, who they would invite. Say that you're going to hear about a dinner party in today's reading and encourage them to listen out to who was invited. Also say that you need their help to tell the story by moving the figures around.

You will need DUPLO (Lego may be a bit small) or PLAYMOBIL® figures, or small dolls to place around two tables, which can either be PLAYMOBIL® versions or made out of card (in proportion to your figures). Read Matthew 9:9–11 from a child-friendly Bible followed by an explanation in your own words of verses 12 and 13. Sit the children round in a rectangle as though sitting at a table so that they can all see and help to place the figures to represent Jesus, Matthew, four of his friends and two Pharisees. Using the *Inventor's Sheets*, invite the children to draw a circle or small picture of Matthew and Jesus at the dining table and then do the same for Jesus' friends and the Pharisees. As they do this, encourage the children to think about the different characters. Did Matthew get up and follow Jesus straightaway? Were the people invited to Matthew's party nice people to have as friends or the sort of people others didn't like? What did Jesus think of them? Now talk about where the children would put themselves in the story. Finish by inviting the children to circle the eight differences in the 'spot the difference'.

With all ages
Adapt these questions to suit your group, sharing your own feelings, opinions and experiences as appropriate:

- Do you think Jesus knew much about Matthew or was this the first time they had met?
- How do you think the tax collectors and sinners felt when Jesus said he came to invite sinners to be his followers?
- Who are the people you know who others don't like much? What could you do to show them kindness?
- What have you learnt about God from today's story?

Power tool (prayer)
Arrange everyone as though they are sitting round a table. Ask each child to say how they are different from others in the group. Encourage them to think of as many differences as possible (eg gender, height, skin, eye and hair colour, families, glasses, different abilities etc). The amazing thing is that Jesus sends out his invitation wider and wider to include everyone who is in the Toolshed. Make sure that the children know each other's names. Invite each child to go round and say the following: Thank you, Jesus, that I am different from X (the child on their right) because… Thank you, Jesus, that you love them.

Construction
Choose a construction activity from pages 63 to 67. For extra craft ideas, see *Ultimate Craft* (SU 978 1 84427 364 5).

Games
Help the Mechanics shape up by choosing suitable games from pages 67 to 69. For more games ideas see *Ultimate Games* (SU 978 1 84427 365 2).

Back to the workshop
25 minutes

Brainbox
Welcome everyone back together by playing the **Mega Makers!** theme song, then hold up the bowl of dough from the messy game so the children can see how much it has expanded.

There will not be many jokes, messages, pictures and questions in the Brainbox today apart from those the team has produced in advance or the children have written or drawn during the session so you might want to have a couple up your sleeve. Encourage children to bring their contributions, but also to bring any inventions they have created. There will be an opportunity to demonstrate these in following sessions.

Music makers

Innovation lead the children in a couple of lively songs.

Drama: Professor Ventor's Miracle Matter-Maker

Introduce the comedy-drama, 'Professor Ventor's Miracle Matter-Maker'. It's an exciting day for the professor, ROBOT and May Kamess, as they prepare to enrol four new apprentices to their workshop. But the applicants aren't quite what Ian Ventor had expected and one of them is a decidedly suspicious character.

Wide, wide world

Jesus invites people from all over the world to become his followers. His invitation gets **wider and wider**. It would therefore be appropriate to pray for a part of the world where people need to hear that Jesus loves them. This might be somewhere in the news right now or it could be a project overseas that your church is involved in. Show some pictures on the screen of the situation giving an explanation to children who do not come to your church. Talk about how you might pray for this situation and then pray simply, explaining that if the children agree with what you say, they should say 'Amen'. Encourage the children to close their eyes since it helps them to concentrate and to put their hands in a position where they can keep them still – on their knees or folding their arms.

Bench test

Rivers get **wider and wider** as they come close to the sea.

How many rivers can the children name? If they run out of rivers they know, they can ask their Engineers. (Write them down and give one point for each answer.)

Alternatively, write out the names of 6 to 10 well-known and local rivers leaving a blank for the vowels. Split the room in half. Taking each half in turn, children suggest a vowel until they work out the name of a river.

Final question: what are the **Mega Makers!** words for today? Use the key words to summarise the story and to reinforce what the children have learnt and discovered about Jesus.

Fusion finale

Round off Back to the workshop by asking two children to say in one sentence what one thing they will share when they get home. Children are used to doing this in school. Leaders can ask a similar question when the children are back in their Toolsheds.

Boffin reminds everyone about the collection procedure, and assures them that he looks forward to seeing them the next day. What will Boffin and Brainwave want to enlarge next in the Mega Machine? What will the apprentices get up to in the drama tomorrow? Then send the children back to their Toolsheds.

Clocking off
10 minutes

If you have a tape measure, the children can work out who has the widest stretch of legs – and getting wider! Make sure that children have what they need to take home, including any construction items they have made. Ask the children what one thing they are going to share about **Mega Makers!** when they get home.

Workshop clear-up
30 minutes

Once the children have gone, tidy up and do any necessary preparation for the following day. As many as possible in the team should meet to debrief on how the first day has gone, identify any hitches that could be put right or any children who have been unhappy.

Report back on how children and leaders in each Toolshed have settled and pray together. Remember to acknowledge and affirm team members' contribution to the session. If possible, share a meal together, although you may only wish to do that on the last day.

DAY 2 THE TRUST IN JESUS

Deeper & deeper

Key passage
Matthew 8:23–27

Key storylines

- Matthew tells the story of Jesus getting into the boat and the disciples following him, which is not how Mark begins the story in Mark 4:35–41. Matthew draws out important lessons about what it means to be a follower of Jesus.

- In desperation, as the storm roars and rages, the disciples wake the sleeping Jesus, who, after challenging them about their lack of trust in him (unlike in Mark), calms the storm. The disciples are so shocked that they wonder just who Jesus is.

- The Machine is not working properly. In frustration Brainwave throws his drink into it and out comes a bucketful of water. Water is in evidence throughout this session.

Key aims

- To welcome each child back to the club, extending a special welcome to anyone who has come for the first time.

- To help children grasp that being a follower of Jesus means that our trust in him gets **deeper and deeper** all the time. Sometimes this just means enjoying being with Jesus, but in the tough times we discover that we can trust him more and more.

- Throughout this programme the children will be discovering more about Jesus as a person. Today they will hear how he has control over creation, the world that he himself made.

- To enable children to see the increasing depth of God's love for them.

For children with no church background

The story of Jesus calming the storm is one of the better-known miracles but it is something of a mystery. It is hard to imagine how one man can stand up in a boat, shout at a storm and it stops! The fact that Jesus was part of the creation process in creating sea, wind and storm is the reason why he could do this. Children with no church background will not have much grasp of Jesus as God in human form. Today's programme will open that up for them a bit more.

Matthew's stress on the effect that Jesus' calming of the storm had on his followers needs careful explanation. Pay special attention to what it actually means to follow Jesus, but not in the way that Brainwave tries to follow Boffin. Also explain the different ways in which we use the word 'deeper' which is central to this day's programme – see page 39. Encourage children to ask questions in their Toolsheds, since it is there that each child's specific questions can be addressed.

For church children

Many children who are part of a church community will say in a bored voice, 'I know this story!' But they have never engaged with it before at this specific point in their lives – and incidentally, it has never featured in a published SU holiday club programme. While we are acknowledging the questions about Jesus' identity, we are focusing more on what Matthew is communicating about discipleship. Following Jesus is far more than just what we say, or just 'how it is

in our family', for it affects every area of life – thoughts, relationships, behaviour, plans for the future, dreams. The Jesus we follow is at the centre of everything. Pray that God's Spirit will be very present with church children and that they will be able to explain to friends what it means to follow Jesus.

For children with other faiths

Historically, in Judaism, the sea has always represented chaos, and been antithetical to God. Holding power over the sea would be an awesome indication of having godlike abilities. In Islam, the seas are within the creation of Allah, so only someone blessed by him would have the power to pray and still it. Within Hinduism, there is a god of the sea, Varuna, but many Hindus only honour a small number of gods, and the most theologically educated (unlikely in young children) recognise only one god, with different aspects represented by different 'gods'. All faiths would recognise the special nature of a man able to command the wind and sea.

For children with additional needs

For some children with ASD or learning difficulties, it may help them to better understand 'deeper and deeper' by adding 'more and more' when following up the teaching.

Action songs and games can be difficult for some children with physical difficulties. Chat with them and find ways to make these songs and games accessible but just as enjoyable.

Engineers' briefing

Spiritual preparation
Read Matthew 8:23–27

Day 2 is always that bit more relaxed since the holiday club has got underway after weeks of preparation and the children will be familiar with the 'routine' of the club. Was that how Jesus' disciples were when they got into the boat in Matthew 8:23, confident and relaxed? Ask the team to think about this as you read Matthew 8:23–27 together. Draw attention to the way the disciples followed Jesus and then left him to go to sleep. Discuss together how the confidence of the disciples was shaken and then partially restored. How would team members have reacted if they had been there?

What would you have said about Jesus if the disciples had asked you, 'What kind of man is this? Even the wind and the waves obey him!'? Share together the characteristic of Jesus that is most significant to you at this particular time and offer a couple of suggestions to give less experienced team members an idea of the type of characteristics you are thinking of – his power, his humanity and normality etc. Share together how your understanding of and relationship with Jesus has got deeper and deeper over the last few months.

Get into small groups and pray for individual children now that leaders have met the children. Pray also for any new children who arrive and for one another. Conclude by singing, 'Jesus, be the centre' or something similar.

Practical preparation

Talk through your programme together. Remind everyone about the key learning aims and who is doing what, ensuring that everyone knows their part in the day and has everything they need. Pay particular attention to younger team members or those who have not been involved before and may be feeling a bit uncertain. Encourage them over the course of the session. This may be the role of the overall leader or could be assigned to another member of the team, or member of the church whose sole role is to encourage the team. Create an atmosphere so that people feel able to ask about anything they are not 100 per cent clear about.

Set up the different areas of the club and make sure that everything is in place in plenty of time, so you are ready as the first children come from the registration area. Leaders need to be especially welcoming to parents and children who have not

Remember that not all disabilities are obvious – some with ADHD or dyspraxia will struggle with jumping, hopping and spinning.

For all-ability parachute games, Through the Roof has a book of these, one of which covers today's story. It also contains good advice on making parachute games inclusive. (*Parachute Bible stories*, ISBN 978 0 95579 642 5; http://youth.throughtheroof.org/parachute-bible-resources)

What-you-need checklist
You will need:

- [ ] **Registration**: registration forms etc, badges, labels, pens, team lists
- [ ] **The Mega Machine**: a fishing net, toy boat, washing-up bottle filled with water, plastic floor covering
- [ ] **The Brainbox**: for jokes, messages, questions and pictures
- [ ] **Messy mechanics**: plastic clear beakers filled with coloured water and a bucket (one for each team)
- [ ] **Technology**: PA system, laptop, PowerPoints and projection/OHP and acetates, **Mega Makers!** DVD
- [ ] **Toolsheds**: materials for mini machines, and opening and closing activities; Bibles, *Inventor's Notebook* or *Inventor's Sheet*, a bucket of water, pebbles or small sinkable objects
- [ ] **Music**: Innovation band or backing tracks
- [ ] **Drama**: costumes and props
- [ ] **Activities**: equipment for games and construction
- [ ] **Boffin and Brainwave** (presenters): running order, equipment for the Mega words, the Learn and remember verse, praying for the wide world, quiz questions
- [ ] **From the Maker's Manual**: story script, a long rope or masking tape
- [ ] **Down tools**: Drinks and biscuits or other refreshments

PHASE 4

37

been before or any adults accompanying children who look uncomfortable being in a church setting. As this is the second day, most people will know what the format is so will be more relaxed.

Listen to any last-minute information or instructions from Boffin and Brainwave, or from the drama, music or refreshment team.

Programme

Clocking in
10 minutes

Make sure the registration team is ready to greet and register the children so that any new children and parents don't have to wait long. Have a welcome team on hand to take the children to their Toolsheds.

It is important that children can identify with their Toolshed leaders who will be with them all the time of the club. Relationship-building and trust begins as soon as each child is welcomed into the Toolshed! These first few minutes are vitally important. Make sure you are familiar with the names of expected children and use the name of each child as much as you can. Introduce unknown children to one another and begin to decorate your Toolshed and make your mini-machine unique to your group of children. For ideas of how to do this, see page 17.

Alternatively, have a couple of yoyos for the children to have a go at propelling something downwards. How long can they keep it up? You could time this unless you have a child who can keep going for ten minutes! Or you could devise a flat target on cardboard or cloth with several numbered circles. Children stand upright on a chair and drop a bean bag or a strong plastic bag filled with water onto the target and score accordingly. The circles should be larger than the bean bag or water bag. Both these games will introduce the idea of depth and objects falling below us.

The inventor's workshop
45 minutes all together

Once all the children are settled in the workshop, Boffin and Brainwave reintroduce themselves, setting the slapstick tone to the programme.

Stretch inventions
Elastic Eureka calls three leaders or older children to the front having primed them to invent a body position which they can hold in a frozen position for 15 seconds and which is physically possible for younger children. Two leaders could devise a position together, such as one leader touches his toes with one hand but puts the other behind his back. The other leader places her hand on his head, slides one leg out in front of her as far as she can go with the other arm held out straight. Each child or pair has to attempt to copy this invented position and then hold it for 15 seconds (or longer if the children are able to sustain it.) Play a stretch invention jingle while the children 'stretch'.

Mega Machine
Brainwave comes in with a bottle/carton of drink – he needs a small amount left by the end of the session to throw into the Mega Machine. Boffin assisted by Brainwave has invented the Mega Machine but it is being rather temperamental. Both of them are very frustrated. They turn it on, in the approved manner. They want to go fishing because Brainwave has decided that he likes fish more than any other food in the world. They have a fishing net, but need a large enough boat for the two of them. Brainwave has found a toy sailing boat and they decide that the Mega Machine will provide them with their very own sailing boat. Carefully Brainwave places the boat into the Mega Machine carrying out all the other procedures necessary to set it in motion. But nothing happens. Boffin looks really worried while Brainwave gets more and more frustrated. In anger he throws the remains of his drink into the Mega Machine, which suddenly bursts into action. Out of it comes a spurt of water, from a washing-up liquid bottle which can be effectively directed! Children love being showered with water but many

will not want to be soaked. Brainwave is sorrowful that he cannot have his fish.

Messy mechanics
In advance, put some plastic sheeting on the floor. Invite several volunteers, possibly one from each Toolshed, to come to the front. Each is given a tablespoon and a transparent plastic beaker containing an equal amount of coloured drink placed on a low table. (Water is less visible from the back of a room.) At least ten metres away, equally accessible to each child, is a large bucket. The volunteers have to gather the liquid on their spoon, place their beaker back on the table, run to the bucket and standing up straight, pour the liquid into the bucket. (This develops the idea of something dropping.)The aim of the race is to see who can empty their beaker first.

Alternatively, three volunteers could each do this one at a time, timing to see who is the fastest. The children can try to make the volunteer laugh or can cheer on their candidate!

Music makers
Get Innovation to remind the children of the **Mega Makers!** theme song and sing it again. Add other songs, mostly repeating those from yesterday, but perhaps introducing one new one. If some children already know a song, get them to come out and help teach it to the others, especially if it has actions or dance movements.

From the Maker's Manual
Boffin walks around saying how glad he is that so many children have come back to have a look at the Machine. He's sorry that it didn't produce the fishing boat but maybe another time. As he is talking, Brainwave is walking behind him, following him and getting in the way. He asks Brainwave what he is doing. Brainwave replies that he is being a follower. Isn't that what followers do, walk in the footsteps of someone they admire? That reminds Boffin of the story where Jesus shows his disciples something about what it means to be one of his followers which the storyteller is going to share with you all.

Storytelling options

Each day, there are three options suggested for telling the Bible story: you can use the same approach each time, mix and match how you tell the story, or combine two or more approaches. Choose which will be most helpful for your team, your children and the style of your club.

- The storyteller tells the story based on Matthew 8:23–27 using their own words if possible (see page 7 for tips on how to do this). You can use the section headings and interactive ideas from the script (see option 3) as memory joggers and to vary your story presentation each time.
- Introduce today's episode from the **Mega Makers!** DVD. (If you are telling the story and using the DVD, tell the story first, then show the DVD so the children already have the outline of the events before seeing the episode.) In today's DVD episode we visit the National Marine Aquarium which is home to some of the most amazing species of fish and sea creatures imaginable. It is in this setting that we'll consider how human achievement has enabled us to dive to greater depths, and to explore the oceans in ways that would have never been thought possible until recently. We'll also think about how deep the oceans are, and against this background explore the depth of God's love. Staying with a related theme, Bob will tell the story of Jesus calming the storm, and help us remember how Jesus can be trusted when we are scared or in danger.
- Or the storyteller may prefer to follow the fully scripted retold Bible story for Day 2 on pages 71 and 72.

Storytelling method: miming team members
The storyteller needs to make sure they are familiar with the script so that they can tell the story fluently and as appropriate in their own words, maintaining eye contact with the children. The storyteller is wearing wellington boots and has an umbrella because there is so much water around.

You will need:
- a long rope or masking tape already stuck to the floor to make the outline of a fishing boat
- four leaders to play the parts of Jesus and three disciples

Mega words

'DEEPER AND DEEPER – the trust in Jesus'

Each day has a key phrase (which is in two parts, the 'expanding words', and the subject of expansion). This will help children to remember what they have learnt and will keep leaders focused on the message they want children to learn. Today's words need to be written vertically on one long strip of paper which is curled up. If your Machine is tall, Brainwave can stand on it to unfurl the words as they sink lower and lower, deeper and deeper. Someone may need to help unroll the Mega words. Alternatively, Brainwave can stand on a ladder or something tall. Ask the children to repeat the words several times.

If any Mechanics have played with a yoyo or dropping bags onto a target you will want to refer to this. Explain that we use the concept of depth to refer to water (the deep end of the swimming pool), a well, a mine or anything that goes down or is dropped. We measure furniture by its height, width and depth. But we also use the word in relationships, in that we talk about loving someone more and more, falling deeper and deeper in love or learning to trust someone more deeply. This is how we are using 'deeper and deeper' at **Mega Makers!**

Ask an engineer

Find a leader who has a love for a particular band or hobby that has grown deeper over the years. First Boffin asks them how far they can stretch to touch the ground, without bending their knees. Initially they do not manage this very well but after several tries and much huffing and puffing they manage to touch their toes and even the ground. They have stretched further and further, deeper and deeper.

Ask the leader what band they admire or hobby they love to do. How long have they taken an interest in this? Has their love for this grown deeper and deeper over the months/years? Boffin comments on this, then asks how far this leader's love for Jesus has got deeper and deeper over the months/years and asks them to elaborate. How much has God's love for them grown? The interviewee needs to use language that is jargon-free and accessible to children. This naturally leads onto the Learn and remember verse.

Learn and remember verse

'I pray that you, together with all God's people, may have the power to understand how broad and long, how high and deep, is Christ's love.'

Ephesians 3:18 (GNB)

Each day explain a bit more of what this verse means. Provide lots of opportunities for children individually and as a group to demonstrate that they have learnt it, with a suitable reward. This verse helps children grasp that Jesus' love is far beyond what any of us can understand but God gives us the power to begin to grasp and experience God with us.

Explain that Paul was writing to a whole load of people who loved Jesus. Being a follower of Jesus means that we belong to a larger group and that we learn to stick together and help each other to find out more about God and to live in a way that pleases him. We are all 'God's people'. With the children's help, work out hand signs for the key words in the first part of verse 18 – you have already taught them the second part. For example, the sign for 'God's people' could be everyone gets in a huddle with their arms around everyone else in the huddle.

Explain that the apostle Paul wanted the Christians in Ephesus, indeed everyone who follows Jesus, to grasp just how great God's love is for them. The more they understood, the more they would realise just how deep his love is, and getting deeper and deeper. In turn, their love for him would get deeper and deeper.

Use the Learn and remember song to reinforce this.

PHASE 4

Power drill
45 minutes in small groups

Down tools
Make sure children are comfortable in their Toolsheds, as they settle for their refreshments. Younger children can take longer over this, so you may want to begin talking about the story as they drink their drinks.

Bible discovery
With older children (8–11s)
Ask the children if they've ever been on a boat trip where the water was really choppy and the waves were really high. Did the waves ever come over the top of the boat? Read Matthew 8:23–27 on page 17 of *Inventor's Notebook*. If you have competent readers in your group ask if one would like to be the narrator, another to be Jesus and another to be the disciples. How do the disciples' feelings change in this story? Get the children to put a number in each box on page 17 to link the feeling with the verse.

Invite responses to the two questions on page 19. (Children may have several answers for both questions. Affirm all of them unless they are really off the wall. We actually don't know how it was that Jesus could sleep but we do know he was not afraid. As for the disciples, maybe this was the first time they were in need or they thought they knew how to sail a boat in the worst of storms and were humiliated or maybe they just did not know enough about Jesus.) Talk about what the children have learnt about Jesus from this passage. Ensure that it is clear that it was because Jesus created the world and was God himself that he could command the storm to be still.

Read out the four things the disciples discovered about being followers of Jesus, from page 19. Talk about times when the children have needed to trust Jesus and be prepared to give a personal example of when you have allowed your trust in Jesus to go deeper and deeper. Turn to page 20 and ask the children to write or draw one thing they want to thank Jesus for, in one footprint, and one reason why it is a good thing to be a

follower of Jesus, in the other. Finish the session by getting the children to do the 'spot the difference' on page 21 of their booklets.

With younger children (5–8s)
Talk about the fact that we feel different things at different times and that our faces often show what we are feeling. Invite the children to give you a facial expression for some different emotions, eg happy, frightened, sad and anxious. Ask them to think about what the disciples might have been feeling at different times in the story they're now going to hear. Read Matthew 8:23–27 using a child-friendly Bible or retell it with your own words. Give out *Inventor's Sheet 2* from page 84 and identify the feelings shown in the illustrations. Then invite the children to number them according to the order of events.

Wonder together about how Jesus could be asleep while the furious storm was raging and draw out the fact that Jesus was not afraid. Also ensure that children understand it was because Jesus created the world and was God himself that he could command the storm to be still. Ask the children what they would have wanted to say to Jesus after he had calmed the storm, if they'd been there.

Talk a bit about how Jesus wanted the disciples to follow him and he wants us to follow him too. This means we know Jesus is with us, he can make a difference in difficult times and we can be thankful to Jesus and praise him for what he does. On the *Inventor's Sheet* there are two large footprints. Ask the children to write or draw one thing they want to thank Jesus for and one reason why it is a good thing to be a follower of Jesus.

With all ages
Adapt these questions to suit your group, sharing your own feelings, opinions and experiences as appropriate:

- What was troubling the disciples and who did they turn to?
- Is there anything that really worries you, makes you afraid or seems impossible?
- Do you think God can help you with this?

Power tool
You will need: a bucket of water; small pebbles or a set of objects such as toy bricks that sink.

Give out the objects and ask each child to think of something for which they want to say thank you to Jesus. As each child shares their cause for thanks, they drop the object deep into the water. Close by thanking Jesus that his love for us is so deep and that he wants us to love him more and more deeply.

Construction
Choose a construction activity from pages 63 to 67. For extra craft ideas, see *Ultimate Craft* (SU 978 1 84427 364 5).

Games
Help the Mechanics shape up by choosing suitable games from pages 67 to 69. For more games ideas see *Ultimate Games* (SU 978 1 84427 365 2).

Back to the workshop
25 minutes

Brainbox
Edit the contributions in the Brainbox today so that you read out the better jokes and messages and answer the important questions. Marvel at any inventions that children have brought to show everyone else. Encourage children to continue to bring their jokes, questions, messages, pictures and inventions they have created.

Music makers
Innovation lead the children in a couple of lively songs

Drama: Professor Ventor's Miracle Matter-Maker
Introduce the next episode of the comedy-drama, 'Professor Ventor's Miracle Matter-Maker'. Today the professor plans to make the final revisions to the Mechanical Miracle Matter-Maker. But suddenly disaster strikes. How will Saw, Claw, Bore, May and ROBOT respond to the crisis? Let's find out.

Wide, wide world

Jesus invites his followers to trust him **more and more deeply**. It would be appropriate to pray for anyone you know who is fearful or a place in the world where people are afraid or pray for children who are starting at a new school and may be apprehensive or those who are moving or facing something else that is new.

Bench test

We say that the stars and planets are **deep** in the universe.

How many stars and planets can the children name? They can ask their Engineers to help them. (Write them down and give one point for each answer.)

Alternatively, write out the names of 6–10 planets and stars leaving a blank for the vowels. Split the room in half. Taking each half in turn, children suggest a vowel until they work out the name of a planet or star.

Final question: what are the Mega words for today? Use the key words to summarise the story and to reinforce what the children have learnt and discovered about Jesus.

Fusion finale

Round off Back to the workshop by asking two children to say in one sentence what one thing they will share when they get home. Children are used to doing this in school. Leaders can ask a similar question when the children are back in their Toolsheds.

Boffin reminds everyone about the collection procedure, and assures them that he looks forward to seeing them the next day. Will the Mega Machine give Boffin the boat he wanted? Will the professor's pants be fixed and will he remember the name of his invention? Then send the children back to their Toolsheds.

Clocking off
10 minutes

If you have a tape measure, the children can work out who has the longest legs, so can stretch down the furthest in the group! Make sure that children have what they need to take home. Ask the children what one thing they are going to share about **Mega Makers!** when they get home.

Workshop clear-up
30 minutes

Once the children have gone, tidy up and do any necessary preparation for the following day. As many as possible in the team should meet to debrief on how the day has gone, identify any hitches that could be put right or any children who have been unhappy, report back on how children and leaders in each Toolshed have been today and spend time praying together. Remember to acknowledge and affirm team members' contribution to the session. If possible, share a meal together, although you may only wish to do that on the last day.

PHASE 4

DAY 3 THE POWER OF JESUS

Stronger&stronger

Key passage
Matthew 9:18,19,23–26

Key storylines

- Matthew's version of the story when Jesus brought a young girl back to life is starkly briefer than Luke's or Mark's. Unlike in Mark, Matthew begins with the girl already dead. Her father exercises great faith in coming to Jesus and asks him to come and simply touch his daughter. He obviously trusts that Jesus' power can make her live.
- The story of the woman bleeding has not been included even though her condition and healing plays a central part in the biblical account.
- The Machine is not ejecting the enlarged objects with enough power so Boffin decides to make some adjustments to increase the power of expulsion.

Key aims

- To welcome each child back to the club, extending a special welcome to anyone who has come for the first time.
- To explore the different meanings of the word 'power' and how Jesus' power is not really about physical force but is more to do with enabling God to make a difference to people's lives.
- To help children grasp that being a follower of Jesus means that we want God to give us the power to understand, know and follow him.
- Throughout **Mega Makers!** the children will discover more about Jesus as a person. Today they will hear how his power brought a girl back to life again.
- To enable children to see the increasing depth of God's love for them.

For children with no church background

This story is not particularly well-known and might make some children feel scared, since many adults are reluctant to talk about the subject of death and dying. Of course, there may be children (and leaders) present who are facing bereavement at the time of the holiday club, so special sensitivity is necessary. The death of a child is particularly shocking in the twenty-first century but it would be less so at the time of Jesus. To avoid the topic though is to deny children the opportunity of talking about death in a safe place.

The leader of the synagogue had a remarkable trust that Jesus could do something about his dead daughter! His faith was strong (and so we are not talking about 'power' as physical strength). He simply asked Jesus to help. All children can discover that they can talk with God about anything and can simply ask, even plead, for him to act and make a difference. But Jesus' power was strong too! Strength has many different meanings, just as God's power can be understood in a variety of ways. As in the last two sessions, children with no church background will discover more about Jesus as God in human form.

For church children

Church children may have had more exposure to the subject of death and dying since one of the great benefits of being in a church community is that children encounter a wider variety of life experiences than the average child does. However do not assume that children

from church are comfortable with talking about death. All children may have lots of questions to ask about what happened, why and so on. Be as open as you can with them. To expand their grasp of the story you could look at the other Gospel accounts (Mark 5:21–43 and Luke 8:40–56), although these are longer than Matthew's version and the story of the woman with the bleeding is included.

Being a follower of Jesus means that God's power, by his Spirit, is at work in us. The Learn and remember verse brings this out in that we need God's power to help us understand God, and to know the vastness of his love for us. Pray that God's Spirit will be very present with church children and that they will experience God's strong power in their lives.

For children with other faiths

Muslims accept Jesus (Isa in Arabic) as a prophet of Allah and, if they believe this account, will ascribe the power to Allah. There are no stories in the Qur'an of Mohammed performing similar miracles. Jewish children might recall that in their Scriptures the prophet Elijah raised a child to life after praying (1 Kings 17:7–24), so you could build on the continuity by asking if Jesus is more than a prophet. For Hindu and some Buddhist children, they may be aware of reincarnation as an expectation of what happens after death, so it might be important to emphasise that this is the same girl in the same body.

Engineers' briefing

Spiritual preparation

Read Matthew 9:18,19, 23–26.

Ask who was exerting power at any one time in the story – Jesus, the religious leader, the mourners? And what sort of power was in evidence? Ultimately it is God's power that can bring people to life, although Jesus' resurrected body was different from the body of the girl. But the father's faith enabled Jesus to exercise his power. It is God's power that will transform people's lives, enabling them to be followers of Jesus and to understand Christ's love – see the Learn and remember verse. All this is somewhat different from physical power and force. As you work through this, talk about what God's power actually means to you. Engineers will need to think about how to explain this in order to help children understand Jesus' power and love.

Pray today for God's power to be at work in the lives of the children, enabling them to understand and grasp his love for them. Pray too that you will see evidence of God at work in other ways too.

Practical preparation

Talk through your programme together. Remind everyone about the key learning aims and who is doing what, ensuring that everyone knows their part in the day and has everything they need. Create an atmosphere so that people feel able to ask about anything they are not 100 per cent clear about.

Set up the different areas of the club and make sure that everything is in place in plenty of time, so you are ready as the first children come from the registration area. Leaders need to be especially welcoming to parents and children who have not been before or any adults accompanying children who look uncomfortable being in a church setting. As this is the third day, most people will know what the format is so will be more relaxed.

For children with additional needs

Your group may include children with visual difficulties. For partially-sighted children, make sure that anything put onto an overhead screen can be reproduced on paper or in a suitable format for an iPad in an appropriate sans serif font of least 18pt. For children with no sight, find a buddy who can adequately describe what is going on for them. Let them feel any puppets or props that are used. You can contact Torch Trust for advice on producing braille (www.torchtrust.org). Provide simple, tactile crafts. These could include ripping and scrunching things for an all together mega craft.

Because of today's story, try to be aware of children struggling with bereavement, or those who have life-limiting disorders and their siblings.

What-you-need checklist

You will need:

- [ ] **Registration**: registration forms etc, badges, labels, pens, team lists
- [ ] **The Mega Machine**: 3 small balls and 3 similar larger balls
- [ ] **The Brainbox**: for jokes, messages, questions and pictures
- [ ] **Messy mechanics**: a large round balloon (one for each team), a tape measure or a long coloured piece of wool
- [ ] **Technology**: PA system, laptop, PowerPoints and projection/OHP and acetates, **Mega Makers!** DVD
- [ ] **Mega words**: balloons with words on blown up
- [ ] **Toolsheds**: materials for mini-machines and opening and closing activities, Bibles, *Inventor's Notebooks* or *Inventor's Sheets*
- [ ] **Music**: Innovation band or backing tracks
- [ ] **Drama**: costumes and props
- [ ] **Activities**: equipment for games and construction
- [ ] **Boffin and Brainwave** (presenters): running order, equipment for Mega words, the Learn and remember verse, praying for the wide world, quiz questions
- [ ] **From the Maker's Manual**: story script, team members to mime the eight actions
- [ ] **Down tools**: Drinks and biscuits or other refreshments

Listen to any last-minute information or instructions from Boffin and Brainwave, or from the drama, music or refreshment teams.

PHASE 4

Programme

Clocking in
10 minutes

Make sure the registration team is ready to greet and register the children so that any new children and parents don't have to wait long. The welcome team can take children to their Toolsheds.

It is important that children can identify with their Toolshed leaders who will be with them all the time of the club. Relationship-building and trust begins as soon as each child is welcomed into the Toolshed group! These first few minutes are vitally important. Use the name of each child as much as you can. Introduce unknown children to one another and continue to decorate your Toolshed and make your mini-machine unique to your group of children. For ideas of how to do this, see page 17.

Alternatively, encourage children to engage in arm wrestling to identify the champion arm-wrestler. Draw up a grid with each child's name on both axes, to record the outcome of each 'bout' of wrestling. Children who do not want to participate can keep the score. What sort of power is being used here? Can the children think of other sorts of power?

The inventor's workshop
45 minutes all together

Once all the children are settled in the workshop, Boffin and Brainwave reintroduce themselves, setting the slapstick tone to the programme.

Stretch inventions

Elastic Eureka calls three leaders or older children to the front having primed them to invent a body position which they can hold in a frozen position for 15 seconds (or longer if the children are able to sustain it) and which is physically possible for younger children. Since Jesus simply touched the girl in the story, their movements could reflect this as hands stretch out as far as possible to lightly touch someone else. Alternatively, if space allows, children could make as large a circle as possible with everyone stretching out arms and legs to touch the person next to them. How big a circle can be made? Play a stretch invention jingle while the children 'stretch'.

Mega Machine

Boffin, assisted by Brainwave, has invented the Mega Machine but it is still not quite as Boffin would like. When the water burst out of the Mega Machine from the previous day he decided that he would like to improve the way the enlarged object bursts powerfully out of the Mega Machine rather than just popping out. He wants something like a cannon ball effect! Brainwave turns on the Mega Machine, in the approved manner. Boffin places a small ball into it and in due course a larger identical ball plops out of the exit. But this is not to Boffin's satisfaction. He wants power! He turns some knobs or rearranges part of the Machine. They try again. This time the larger ball comes out with a bit more force, but it is only on the third time that it bursts out. Boffin is satisfied. He and Brainwave reflect on different ways of understanding 'power' – physical strength, might, force, energy, authority, potential, quiet control, aptitude, personal charisma. Explain that very soon you will be exploring what sort of power Jesus had.

Messy mechanics

One child from each Toolshed comes to the front. Each blows up one balloon as large as they can, but holds their balloon at the end to prevent air coming out. The children stand in a row and in turn let go of their balloon to see which balloon flies the furthest. You could measure the distance by a tape measure or just a piece of coloured wool. The balloons can go off in any direction. Reward in some way the Toolshed that wins. Remind the children that power from the lungs is needed to force air into a balloon and then as the air is forced out, the balloon itself is propelled through the air.

Music makers

Reintroduce Innovation and use mostly songs that you have already done with the children, perhaps including another new one, especially if some of the children could help the others to learn it. You could finish with the **Mega Makers!** theme song, and include any actions you might have come up with!

From the Maker's Manual

Brainwave keeps bumping into Boffin and touching his arms, shoulders and forehead. Boffin gets fed up with this but Brainwave cannot help it. He is all over the place today. This reminds Boffin of the story where Jesus takes the hand of a 12-year-old girl who had died.

Storytelling options

Each day, there are three options suggested for telling the Bible story: you can use the same approach each time, mix and match how you tell the story, or combine two or more approaches. Choose which will be most helpful for your team, your children and the style of your club.

◉ The storyteller tells the story based on Matthew 8:23–27 using their own words if possible (see page 7 for tips on how to do this). You can use the section headings and interactive ideas from the script (see option 3) as memory joggers and to vary your story presentation each time.

◉ Introduce today's episode from the **Mega Makers!** DVD. (If you are telling the story and using the DVD, tell the story first, then show the DVD so the children already have the outline of the events before seeing the episode.) In today's DVD episode we'll be at Bug World at Bristol Zoo exploring this fascinating part of God's creation. We'll look at the strength of insects – and see how these have inspired human science and invention. Through this Gemma and Bob will help us see that even small things can be powerful. Out of this, Bob will tell us the story of a man called Jairus, whose little girl was ill, and how, through his hopes in Jesus, God's strength was able to bring healing and life.

◉ Or the storyteller may prefer to follow the fully scripted retold Bible story for Day 3 on page 72.

Storytelling method: eight dramatic actions (performed by a team member). The storyteller needs to make sure they are familiar with the script so that they can tell the story fluently and in their own words, maintaining eye contact with the children.

You will need:

⊙ One leader for each of the four characters to mime the action:

⊙ Leader 1: Jesus, in a simple costume which could be a scarf

⊙ Leader 2: the father, holding a large handkerchief to wipe his eyes

⊙ Leader 3: the daughter wearing a headscarf

⊙ Leader 4: holds up eight large cards, numbered 1–8 with the actions printed out as newspaper headlines as follows:

1 **JESUS** SITS DOWN
2 **FATHER** KNEELS DOWN
3 **FATHER** HOLDS OUT HANDS, PLEADINGLY
4 **JESUS** WALKS WITH FATHER
5 **JESUS** KNOCKS ON DOOR
6 **JESUS** SHOOS MUSICIANS AWAY
7 **JESUS** TAKES GIRL'S HAND
8 **GIRL** GETS UP

There are eight actions to this story (that match these newspaper headlines) and the children need to remember what they all are and the order they come in. Then they can share this story with someone else when they get home. The storyteller relates the story in his own words as the actions take place. Tell the story slowly and simply for dramatic effect.

Mega words

'**STRONGER AND STRONGER** – the power of Jesus'

Each day has a key phrase (which is in two parts: the 'enlarging words', and the subject of expansion). This will help children to remember what they have learnt and will keep leaders focused on the message they want children to learn.

Today's words, 'stronger and stronger', do not imply that Jesus got stronger the longer he lived but that the more people discovered about him, the more they realised that he was God, with all the 'power of God', which he used so sparingly. Children may think of 'power' in terms of Superman or zapping brute force. Jesus' power was much more restrained and controlled.

In advance, blow up seven balloons and write one of these words on each of them – Stronger/and/stronger/the/power/of/Jesus. Put the balloons in a black bin bag and carry it on as if it's really heavy! Ask for seven children to pull out the balloons and put them into an order that makes sense to create today's Mega words.

Ask an engineer

Interview a leader first by asking them to do some mental arithmetic, maybe check on their times table. The children may be able to do this more quickly. Comment on the leader's ability or power to do this. Of course, they may be powerful in other ways – physically strong or have strong powers of concentration.

Ask them about a time when they felt weak and needed to experience the power of God in their life. Make sure that this is an experience that children can identify with, such as a time of illness for them or someone close to them, or a time when they were caught in a difficult situation that they could not see any way out of.

Learn and remember

'I pray that you, together with all God's people, may have the power to understand how broad and long, how high and deep, is Christ's love.'

Ephesians 3:18 (GNB)

Each day explain a bit more of what this verse means. Provide lots of opportunities for children individually and as a group to demonstrate that they have learnt it, with a suitable reward. This verse helps children grasp that Jesus' love is far beyond what any of us can understand but God gives us the power to begin to grasp and experience God with us.

See how many children can remember the verse and the hand signs you used on Day 2. Ask where the word 'power' comes in the verse. What sort of power is Paul referring to? (You may be using a 'power' hand sign of a clenched fist which would suggest physical power. If so, you could change the sign to reflect an 'internal' power such as closing eyes and gently stroking the forehead with both hands, indicating a profound thought process!) It will probably help to explore the children's abilities to understand something that is hard and requires concentration – refer back to the interview with the leader. Paul wanted God's people to have the God-given power themselves to understand more about God, which includes expecting and knowing that Jesus had the power to do some pretty remarkable things.

Use the Learn and remember song to reinforce this.

Power drill
45 minutes in small groups

Down tools

Make sure children are comfortable in their Toolsheds, as they settle for their refreshments. Younger children can take longer over this, so you may want to begin talking about the story as they drink their drinks.

Bible discovery
With older children (8–11s)

Ask the children to think of different ways we talk about someone or something 'being strong', eg can lift heavy things, getting through a difficult time, a strong wind. Read Matthew 9:18,19,23–26 on pages 23 and 24 of *Inventor's Notebook*. If you have competent readers, ask if one would like to be the narrator, another to be Jesus and another to be the father. Encourage the children to fill in who is being strong at each stage of the story, on pages 23 and 24 and talk about whether it's easy or not to be strong in difficult situations. Reassure children that it was more common in those days for children to die and give opportunity for them to ask questions about death and dying but be sensitive to the needs of the group and make sure you also talk about how amazing it was that Jesus brought the girl back to life. Ask the children what sort of power Jesus was using and write their answer in the speech bubble on page 24. Get the children to do the maze on page 25. Go through the three questions on page 26 together, encouraging as many children as possible to participate.

If you used the scripted storytelling method, ask the children if they can remember the eight stages in the story and the actions. Once you have established what they are, you could ask them to act out the story adding extra people and actions. If you have time, get the children to fill in the missing words to the memory verse on page 29. Ask them what they have discovered so far about Jesus' love and power.

With younger children (5–8s)

Talk about the people they think of as 'strong' eg Superman, a weightlifter, their dad. Explain that sometimes we also talk about people being 'strong' when they are brave in a difficult situation.

Ask the children to listen carefully while you read Matthew 9:18,19,23–26 from a child-friendly Bible. As you read ask the children to point to the eight pin men pictures on *Inventor's Sheet 3* on page 85.

Reassure children that it was more common in those days for children to die and give opportunity for them to ask questions about death and dying but be sensitive to the needs of the group and make sure you also talk about how amazing it was that Jesus brought the girl back to life.

Ask the children what sort of strong person they would want to be with them if they are feeling weak, afraid or alone. Talk about how Jesus is with us all the time, including when we don't feel strong.

If you used the scripted storytelling method, run through the eight stages in the story again, and invite the children to act them out.

Get the children to write or draw on the hand image on *Inventor's Sheet 3* something they want to ask Jesus for.

With all ages

Adapt these questions to suit your group, sharing your own feelings, opinions and experiences as appropriate:

- What did Jesus' followers discover about Jesus through this incident?
- What have you discovered today about Jesus' power?
- How can being a friend of Jesus make you strong?

Power tool

You will need a piece of paper on which is one palm-print outline, one for each child. Children could draw round their own hand, to create their own palm outline. A palm outline is also available in *Inventor's Notebook* and the *Inventor's Sheet*. If you are using the hand-print on the *Inventor's Sheet* or in the booklet you will not want to stick the handprint onto a larger hand.

Ask the children where hands come into the story of Jesus and the leader's daughter – the leader pleads with Jesus, Jesus shoos away the musicians, Jesus takes the girl by the hand. Give out the handprints and remind the children that just as the father held out his hands to ask Jesus, so we can ask Jesus to help us. Ask children to write or draw on one palm something they want to ask Jesus for.

If appropriate, children could stick their palm-print onto a much larger hand, for by praying we are placing ourselves in the powerful hands of Jesus who hears our conversation and will act to make a difference. This large hand could be just for children in each Toolshed to use or a really large one could be created and placed in a central place for all the children to stick on their own prayer request some time during the session.

Construction

Choose a construction activity from pages 63 to 67. For extra craft ideas, see *Ultimate Craft* (SU 978 1 84427 364 5).

Games

Help the Mechanics shape up by choosing suitable games from pages 67 to 69. For more games ideas see *Ultimate Games* (SU 978 1 84427 365 2).

Back to the workshop
25 minutes

Brainbox

Edit the jokes, messages, questions and pictures in the Brainbox today. Marvel at any inventions that children have brought to show everyone. Encourage children to bring their jokes, messages, pictures, questions and inventions they have created to post in Brainbox tomorrow.

Music makers

Innovation lead the children in a couple of lively songs

Drama: Professor Ventor's Miracle Matter-Maker

Introduce the next episode of the comedy-drama, 'Professor Ventor's Miracle Matter-Maker. Professor Ian Ventor and ROBOT are busy checking the plans for the Mechanical Miracle Matter-Maker. But Dr O'Good is up to no good. Will he be able to succeed with his dastardly plans? Will May overcome her fear of spiders? Let's find out.

Wide, wide world

The more we discover about Jesus, the more we realise how strong his power is. Ask the children to join hands with those close to them, maybe making one long joined-up chain. Remind them of the place of hands in this story. Pray that you will have God's power to discover just how much he loves us all and how his power can make us brave when we feel weak. Ask the children to be silent for a short while to talk with God themselves. Conclude by praying for anyone known to the children present who is feeling in need of God's power at work in their lives.

Bench test

Write the letters of the word STRENGTH vertically down a large sheet of flip chart paper. Since hands have been part of the story, ask children to give you the names of any parts of the body which begin with any of these letters. Each viable suggestion scores a point. For example:

S stomach, skin, shoulder

T toe, thumb, tongue,

R ribs, ribcage, ring finger, (not wrist), retina

E ear, eye, eyebrow, eyelash, elbow

N neck, nose, nail, (not knee), nostril

G gut, gullet, gum

T tummy, tooth, tibea, tear duct, tonsil

H heart, hand, head, hair, heel

Final question: what are the Mega words for today? Use the key words to summarise the story and to reinforce what the children have learnt and discovered about Jesus.

Fusion finale

Round off Back to the workshop by asking two children to say in one sentence what one thing they will share when they get home. Children are used to doing this in school. Leaders can ask a similar question when the children are back in their Toolsheds.

Boffin reminds everyone about the collection procedure, and assures them that he looks forward to seeing them the next day. Will the Mega Machine continue to have extra expulsion power? Have we seen the last of Dr O'Good? Then send the children back to their mini-machines.

Clocking off
10 minutes

You could continue thinking of the names of different parts of the body as you wait for parents and carers to collect their children. Make sure children have what they need to take home. Ask the children what one thing they are going to share about **Mega Makers!** when they get home.

Workshop clear-up
30 minutes

Once the children have gone, tidy up and do any necessary preparation for the following day. As many as possible in the team should meet to debrief on how the session has gone, identify any hitches that could be put right or any children who have been unhappy, report back on how the session in each Toolshed has been and spend time praying

together. Remember to acknowledge and affirm team members' contribution to the session. If possible, share a meal together, although you may only wish to do that on the last day.

PHASE 4

DAY 4 THE LOVE OF JESUS

Greater & greater

Key passage
Matthew 26:36–41,50b,56b; 27: 27–46,50,54

Key storylines
⊙ Matthew's retelling of the crucifixion presents Jesus as someone rejected and scorned. The title JESUS, THE KING OF THE JEWS, pinned above his head, could be seen as a sign that this was a failed king, a victim. But this is far from the truth. Jesus came to die. He made the choice to die, as evidenced by his prayer to his Father in Gethsemane. We need to ensure that children are sad about Jesus' death but do not feel sorry for him. He is victorious.

⊙ Three parts of the story are focused on in the programme: Jesus in the garden of Gethsemane, his disciples deserting him on his arrest, and the crucifixion itself.

⊙ Boffin and Brainwave disagree over what to put in the Machine. Brainwave is so frustrated that he loses his temper. But he comes to realise that Boffin loves him and wants the best for him.

Key aims
⊙ To welcome each child back to the club.
⊙ To help children engage with the story of the crucifixion, seeing how much Jesus suffered but that he was not a victim. He chose to die because he loves us. His love for us is greater than we can ever imagine!
⊙ To challenge children to become lifelong followers of Jesus. To enable children to see the increasing depth of God's love for them.

For children with no church background

The story of the crucifixion is not pleasant. Children may be used to violent images on their screens but this is a particularly vicious story – and without the resurrection, it is a hopeless one. Sensitive children may be disturbed. We need to tell the story clearly, without over-emphasising Jesus' suffering. Ensure children know that Jesus came alive again, even though the final day of the club focuses entirely on the resurrection. As some children may not come for the final session, children with no church background do need to know that his death was not the end.

Explaining the meaning of the cross to any age group is a challenge. It is hard to understand why the death of an innocent man was needed for someone to have a relationship with God. Children are aware of someone being blamed for something wrong and even of someone taking the blame on behalf of someone else. This is the language used in this session. If appropriate give an opportunity to consider becoming a follower of Jesus. Do your best to make it clear to those with no church background what is meant by following Jesus. We do not want them to make some sort of commitment motivated by a desire to please a leader or where you discern they are not yet ready to respond. Pray that God by his Spirit will be active in the lives of all children with no church background, sowing seeds that both you and others will reap in years to come.

For church children

Church children will have heard the story of the crucifixion many times. But this can have the effect of anaesthetising them to its power and significance. They may be able to parrot the phrases 'Jesus died for my sins', or 'Jesus died to save me' but not really experience what it all means for them. This session is an opportunity to deepen not only their understanding of the story but also to consider what it means for them to be a follower of Jesus. One benefit of a holiday club is that it gives scope for more intensive input into the lives of church children than is possible just on a Sunday. Towards the end of this club, children may be particularly open to make an initial or further step of commitment to Christ.

For children with other faiths

Muslims may have been taught that Jesus did not really die, so it may be helpful to a) demonstrate that Roman soldiers were thorough in killing people and b) show the continuity of custody so substituting Jesus' body is unlikely. As with yesterday's story, Hindu and some Buddhist children may need help understanding it is the same person, not a reincarnation. It is also important to put the death firmly into Roman hands, so that Jewish children do not go away thinking their people are 'Christ killers', which historically has led to Jewish persecution by Christians.

Engineers' briefing

Spiritual preparation

Read Matthew 26:36–41, 50b,56b; 27:27–46,50,54

Use the copies of the Bible verses that the children are using. Ask how far people can identify with the different groups in the story – religious leaders, soldiers, the crowd and Jesus' friends. Why did they act as they did towards Jesus?

In small groups ask each leader to think of each of the children in their group. This may be hard, but which group in the story is each child most like? Is there any evidence that a child is not really interested in Jesus (the crowd), opposed to him (the religious leaders), just getting on with life but open to find out more (the soldiers) or Jesus' friends (want to follow Jesus, but sometimes they fail). In the light of this, pray for every child by name. By now, at least one team member should know each child.

Finally, ask your church leader(s), whether or not they are involved in the club, to pray for you all. When the story of the cross is central in a session there is frequently some form of opposition, distraction or something goes wrong. Pray for God's protection and the ability for everyone to clearly explain the meaning of the cross, whether doing it up-front, in the Toolsheds or individually. Encourage everyone to pray for each other throughout the session.

Practical preparation

Talk through your programme together. Remind everyone of the key learning aims and who is doing what, ensuring that everyone knows their part in the day and has everything they need.

Set up the different areas of the club and make sure that everything is in place in plenty of time, so you are ready as the first children come from the registration area. Listen to any last-minute information or instructions from Boffin and Brainwave, or from the drama, music or refreshment teams.

For children with additional needs

Be aware that there may be children who, through difficult home circumstances (now or in the past), find the idea of being loved difficult to comprehend. Trusting will not be easy for them because they feel the need to be in charge of their lives. This is because they believe that it is safer if they can control what happens around them. This is a normal reaction; don't try to force change in this area. You can also help by:

- giving lots of time for questions
- being aware that they may also find the story of the crucifixion more upsetting than others
- being careful of terminology in explaining what a Christian is
- being realistic in what you say happens after choosing to follow Jesus, as these children will have a very black and white view of life.

What-you-need checklist

You will need:

- [ ] **Registration**: registration forms etc, badges, labels, pens, team lists
- [ ] **The Mega Machine**: two objects to throw into the machine such as a doughnut and a turnip
- [ ] **The Brainbox**: for jokes, messages, questions and pictures
- [ ] **Messy mechanics**: two bowls of ice cream or other messy food, plastic covering
- [ ] **Technology**: PA system, laptop, PowerPoints and projection/OHP and acetates, **Mega Makers!** DVD
- [ ] **Mega words**: a large cross; evangelistic booklets
- [ ] **Toolsheds**: materials for mini-machines and opening and closing activities; Bibles, *Inventor's Notebook* or *Inventor's Sheets*
- [ ] **Music**: Innovation band or backing tracks
- [ ] **Drama**: costumes and props
- [ ] **Activities**: equipment for games and construction
- [ ] **Boffin and Brainwave** (presenters): running order, equipment for Mega words, the Learn and remember verse, praying for the wide world, quiz questions
- [ ] **From the Maker's Manual**: story script, five chairs with appropriate phrases on front and back (or large cardboard people), cloth to cover them
- [ ] **Down tools**: Drinks and biscuits or other refreshments

PHASE 4

Programme

Clocking in
10 minutes

Make sure the registration team is ready to greet and register the children.

It is important that children can identify with their Toolshed leaders who will be with them all the time of the club. By now everyone will be familiar with the routine. Children will be looking forward to meeting with others in the Toolshed and hopefully will trust their leaders. Be ready to engage with the children, looking for opportunities to ask them what they are learning and discovering in the club as well as talking with them about Jesus. Continue to decorate your Toolshed and make your mini-machine unique to your group of children. For ideas of how to do this, see page 17.

Alternatively, to introduce the idea of the cross, choose from the following craft ideas: pieces of cross-shaped card that can be decorated – scratch art crosses are a great idea; two pieces of wood that can be bound together with string to form a cross or the materials to make a Mexican cross (search under 'God's eye weave' on the internet). All these can be started at the beginning and completed in the Toolshed time.

The inventor's workshop
45 minutes all together

Once all the children are settled in the workshop, Boffin and Brainwave reintroduce themselves, setting the slapstick tone to the programme.

Stretch inventions
Elastic Eureka calls three leaders or older children to the front having primed them to invent a body position which they can hold in a frozen position for 15 seconds (or longer if the children are able to sustain it) and which is physically possible for younger children. Since the cross is central to this session, can they invent positions which involve crossing... legs, arms, fingers, crossing one another

in pairs or threes? Play a stretch invention jingle while the children 'stretch'.

Mega Machine
The Machine is still not quite as Boffin would like and Brainwave is getting really angry with Boffin. Brainwave wants to insert several objects and Boffin objects to all of them, for good reasons – such as Brainwave loves doughnuts so thinks a giant doughnut would be amazing. Boffin says it would be bad for Brainwave and cannot guarantee that the machine would instead produce lots of mini-doughnuts that could be shared with everyone.

Brainwave then wants to throw in a turnip but Boffin says that he knows that Brainwave does not like turnip (how many of the children do?) so what is the point? Brainwave says they are only testing and he is sure his pet pig likes turnips. But how will Brainwave transport a giant turnip to his home on a bicycle?

Brainwave is so furious with Boffin that he loses his temper and shouts out that he would like to get rid of Boffin and throw him into the Machine. When Brainwave has calmed down and said he is sorry, Boffin dryly suggests that an enlarged Boffin might be even worse than a smaller one. Brainwave asks Boffin why he did not get angry with Brainwave and did not attempt to get rid of him. Boffin replies that he loves Brainwave and wants him to become a great inventor himself. Brainwave is astounded at this. 'How can you love me when I wanted to get rid of you?' he asks. Boffin says that it is all to do with loving someone.

Messy mechanics
Sit two people opposite each other and blindfold them both. Hand one a dish of ice cream and a spoon, and gently tie the other person's hands behind their back (so they can't feel for the spoon and guide it into their mouth). The person with the ice cream must now try to feed the other. If you want to make this more competitive have another pair and score points as to who eats the most ice cream or who gets in the most mess!

Music makers
Reintroduce Innovation and sing the **Mega Makers!** theme song, along with any actions. Sing a song that you have already sung at **Mega Makers!** and introduce a new one today, related to today's theme such as 'Jesus' love is very wonderful'.

From the Maker's Manual
Boffin reminds Brainwave of the question he asked a few minutes ago – 'How can you love me when I wanted to get rid of you?' Boffin says that people wanted to get rid of Jesus, despite all the great things he has said and done. Jesus could have stopped his enemies but he didn't because he loved them. He loved all people. He knew his death could change the world. It is a very sad story, but let the children into a secret. It does have a happy ending!

Storytelling options
Each day, there are three options suggested for telling the Bible story: you can use the same approach each time, mix and match how you tell the story, or combine two or more approaches. Choose which will be most helpful for your team, your children and the style of your club.

- The storyteller tells the story based on Matthew 26:36–41,50b,56b; 27:27–46,50,54 using their own words if possible (see page 7 for tips on how to do this). You can use the section headings and interactive ideas from the script (see option 3) as memory joggers and to vary your story presentation each time.

- Introduce today's episode from the **Mega Makers!** DVD. (If you are telling the story and using the DVD, tell the story first, then show the DVD so the children already have the outline of the events before seeing the episode.) In today's episode of the DVD we'll be on location with some beautiful birds of prey, exploring their ability as aviators and hunters. With footage filmed from the birds themselves, Gemma and Bob will help us to appreciate these incredible inventions of God's creation. Bob will tell the story of how Jesus died, and help us to see that even though people might have thought this was a disaster, when looked at from a different perspective, we can see that God had everything under control.

◉ Or the storyteller may prefer to follow the fully scripted retold Bible story for Day 4 on pages 73 and 74.

Storytelling method: visual aids – moveable chairs

The storyteller needs to make sure they are familiar with the script below so that they can tell the story fluently (in their own words), maintaining eye contact with the children. It would help to practise telling the story with someone else moving the chairs/cardboard people since the story needs to be told fairly briskly.

In advance, print the following words in large type on separate sheets of card:

◉ THE RELIGIOUS LEADERS
◉ JESUS' FRIENDS
◉ SOLDIERS
◉ CROWDS OF PEOPLE
◉ GOD THE FATHER
◉ WANT TO GET RID OF JESUS
◉ WANT TO FOLLOW JESUS BUT …..
◉ IT'S OUR JOB BUT THIS MAN WAS GOD'S SON!
◉ NOT SURE ABOUT JESUS
◉ I LOVE JESUS. HE'S MY SON

Set out five chairs to face the children. Take the first five phrases and attach one to the front of each chair, then attach the next five phrases to the back of each chair keeping the sequence as above. Then cover the chair with a cloth so none of the words are showing. Alternatively, create five large cardboard figures with the words printed on them, front and back.

Mega words
'**GREATER AND GREATER** – the love of Jesus'

Each day has a key phrase (which is in two parts, the 'enlarging words', and the subject of expansion). This will help children to remember what they have learnt and will keep leaders focused on the message they want children to learn.

Write today's words, on the crossbar of a cross, either a large cross that you have

in church or as a PowerPoint. As Jesus hung on the cross his arms were forced out wide. Explain that arms are used to hug and protect people so this action is also symbolic. His arms stretch out wide to embrace anyone who wants to know God, to be a follower of Jesus. This is how great his love is. He was prepared to die for the whole world. Invite the children to stretch their arms out as wide as they can, without poking anyone. Say the Mega words together three times, starting quietly and getting louder and louder.

Ask an engineer
Interview a leader first by asking them to briefly say what it means to them that Jesus loves them. How do they know how great Christ's love is? (see Learn and remember verse.) Encourage them to briefly say how they have come to be a follower of Jesus, being careful to use language that children can understand.

Learn and remember

'I pray that you, together with all God's people, may have the power to understand how broad and long, how high and deep, is Christ's love.'

Ephesians 3:18 (GNB)

By now many of the children will have learnt this verse. Say it together, and then ask the children how great they think Christ's love is. Affirm their answers and then read out verse 19 of Ephesians 3 and talk a bit about how Christ's love is too wonderful to be measured. Refer to the leader's interview and what was said about knowing Christ's love.

Use the Learn and remember verse song, although this does not specifically use the phrase 'Christ's love is greater than anyone can ever know'.

Power drill
45 minutes in small groups

Down tools
Make sure children are comfortable in their Toolsheds, as they settle for their refreshments. Younger children can

take longer over this, so you may want to begin talking about the story as they drink their drinks.

Bible discovery
With older children (8–11s)
Talk together about who the children think are 'great' people; their heroes/ heroines. Ask them what qualities they think someone needs to be great. Read Matthew 26:36–41,50b,56b; 27:27–46,50,54 using pages 30 to 32 of the *Inventor's Notebook*. Now ask the children to read the story again and, using different lines, underline the words written about each of the groups of people.

Explore together what it meant that Jesus was a King of the Jews. It was the Jewish religious leaders who wanted Jesus dead. They did not see him as their king! The sign saying 'King of the Jews' was placed there by Roman soldiers as a warning to everybody that no one could claim to be king while the Romans were in power. But the sign reminds us that Jesus was far more than an earthly king; he was a victorious king. Ask the children to think of an instance when someone has been blamed for something they haven't done. Share any experience you have had of this. Then ask the children how they would feel if someone chooses to take the blame for something they have not done – both from the perspective of the one who takes the blame and the one who should have been blamed. Use this to explain why Jesus chose to die. Emphasise that he did this because he loves all people, those who were alive at the time and people alive today. On page 33, get the children to put a tick against those people they might feel sorry for and a cross beside those people that could have done something differently. (If someone suggests feeling sorry for Jesus, explore the difference between feeling sad and feeling sorry. Jesus was not a victim; he had chosen to do what God his Father wanted. He died because he loved the people of this world.)

Get the children to find all the character names in the wordsearch on page 34 and use the spare letters to fill in the statement below it. Discuss together what things they can do to show love for others, then encourage them to write or draw their ideas in the space on page 37.

Encourage any child who wants to know more about following Jesus to talk with you or suggest who else they might like to talk with.

With younger children (5–8s)

Talk together about who the children think are 'great' people; their heroes/ heroines. Ask them what qualities they think someone needs to be great. Then read Matthew 26:36–41,50b,56b; 27:27–46,50,54 using a child-friendly Bible or retell it with your own words. Give out *Inventor's Sheet 4* and talk about the characters in the story and identify which people are in which illustration. Then ask the children how each of these groups felt about Jesus. They can then colour in the illustrations.

Look at the picture at the bottom of the page and get the children to count up how many cross-shapes they can find. Then talk about how happy Jesus' friends were to see him alive again – say that they'll hear more about that tomorrow.

With all ages

Adapt these questions to suit your group, sharing your own feelings, opinions and experiences as appropriate:
- How does it make you feel that Jesus died for you?
- What have you learnt about God from today's passage?

Power tool

You will need heart-shaped sticky notes. On the sticky note, ask the children to write or draw something they want to say to Jesus about his love. Give them some suggestions.
- Thank him that he loves them so much that he took the blame for their wrongdoing.
- Draw or write the name of someone who needs to know that Jesus loves them.
- Draw a big smile because it makes them happy to know Jesus loves them.
- Draw a sad mouth because they know they have done wrong things which displease God.

- Draw a question mark because they are thoughtful, wanting to find out more.

Depending on what is going to happen in Praying for the world at the end of the session will depend on how you are going to use the sticky notes.

Construction

Choose a construction activity from pages 63 to 67. For extra craft ideas, see *Ultimate Craft* (SU 978 1 84427 364 5).

Games

Help the Mechanics shape up by choosing suitable games from pages 67 to 69. For more games ideas see *Ultimate Games* (SU 978 1 84427 365 2).

Back to the workshop
25 minutes

Brainbox

Edit the jokes, messages, pictures and comments in the Brainbox today. Marvel at any inventions that children have brought to show everyone else. Encourage children to bring their jokes, messages, pictures, questions and inventions they have created tomorrow since there is only one day left of **Mega Makers!**

Music makers

Innovation lead the children in a couple of lively songs.

Drama: Professor Ventor's Miracle Matter-Maker

Introduce the next episode of the comedy-drama, 'Professor Ventor's Miracle Matter-Maker'. There's great excitement in the Professor's workshop as he gets close to completing the Mechanical Miracle Matter-Maker. But while he and May Kamess go off to buy some essential parts, Dr O' Good is once more up to no good. Will he succeed in his plans to sabotage the machine? And what will the Professor's revolting recipe be today? Let's find out.

Wide, wide world

The symbol for love is a heart. Stick a large heart shape onto a board and give

---

each child a heart-shaped sticky note and pen/pencil. Ask them to write or draw something they want to say to Jesus about his love. See suggestions above in Power tool. Children can stick their notes on the large heart.

This may take more than five minutes. Either allow extra time for this or children could write their sticky notes in their Toolsheds and stick it onto the large heart as they gather back in the workshop. If the latter suggestion is followed, Boffin could read out some of the prayers and draw them together in one prayer.

Bench test

Divide the children into two teams. The questions in this quiz are factual with the intention of focusing on the story and the wonder of the greatness of Jesus' love. You may not want to use every question, especially if the answer has not been given in the session.
- What time of the day was Jesus in the vineyard with his friends? Night
- How many of his closest friends did Jesus take to comfort him? Three
- Who were there? Peter, James and John 3 points
- What did his disciples do while Jesus was asking his Father to make it possible for him not to suffer? Fell asleep
- What did his disciples do when Jesus was arrested? Ran away
- What was on the sign above Jesus' head? This is Jesus, the King of the Jews.
- How many criminals were also crucified with him? Two
- What did people and the religious leaders say about Jesus as he hung on the cross? There are several answers which older children will have read in the Bible passage.
- What time did it go dark? 12 noon
- What did Jesus cry from the cross? 'My God, my God, why have you deserted me?'
- What time did Jesus cry this? 3 o'clock in the afternoon
- What did the army officer and the soldiers say after Jesus died? 'He really was God's Son.' Final question: what are the Mega words for today? Use the

key words to summarise the story and to reinforce what the children have learnt and discovered about Jesus.

Fusion finale

Round off Back to the workshop by asking two children to say in one sentence what one thing they will share when they get home. Children are used to doing this in school. Leaders can ask a similar question when the children are back in their Toolsheds.

Boffin reminds everyone about the collection routine, and assures them that he looks forward to seeing them the next day. Will Brainwave be in a better mood tomorrow? What will the professor do if onesies go out of fashion? Then send the children back to their Toolsheds.

Clocking off
10 minutes

Children may need to finish the crosses they started earlier in the session. Make sure that children have what they need to take home. Ask the children what one thing they are going to share about **Mega Makers!** when they get home.

Workshop clear-up
30 minutes

Once the children have gone, tidy up and do any necessary preparation for the following day. As many as possible in the team should meet to debrief on how the session has gone, identify any hitches that could be put right or any children who have been unhappy, report back on how children and leaders in each Toolshed have settled and spend some time praying together. Remember to acknowledge and affirm team members' contribution to the session. If possible, share a meal together, although you may only wish to do that on the last day.

PHASE 4

DAY 5 FRIENDSHIP WITH JESUS

For ever & ever

Key passage
Matthew 28:1–10

Key storylines

◉ Matthew's retelling of Jesus' appearance to the women is different from the other Gospels. There are four component parts – 1) there is an earthquake (the second one that 'weekend' 27:51; 28:2), 2) the angel comes from heaven, removing the stone to reveal an already empty tomb, 3) the effect that this has upon the guard, 4) the women meet Jesus on their way from the tomb.

◉ As you share this story stick to Matthew's version. Tell it simply but with utter conviction. Jesus came alive again! In preparation, read Matthew 27:57 – 28:10 so that you can get the details correct.

◉ Boffin and Brainwave find it hard to believe that the Mega Machine is now working. They put two things into it which come out larger. Such success is worth a celebration!

Key aims

◉ To welcome each child back to the club and give them a memorable final day.

◉ To help children engage with the story of the resurrection. Jesus came alive again and he is still alive with us today.

◉ To awake children to the call to tell others that Jesus is alive, just as Jesus told the women to tell the other followers.

◉ To challenge children to become lifelong followers of Jesus. Jesus will be their friend for ever.

◉ To enable children to see the increasing depth of God's love for them.

For children with no church background

The story of Jesus rising from the dead is a mystery. Allow children with no church background to ask questions and wonder just how it happened. Was Jesus a ghost? How did the women know that it was Jesus? Did the angel let Jesus out of the tomb or had he gone before the angel rolled the stone away? When did Jesus die a second time? Be prepared to explain what it means to you that Jesus came alive again and is with you all the time.

Since you may be seeing some children for the last time, make every effort to draw alongside them to talk about what they have enjoyed about the club and what they have discovered about Jesus. Invite them to any other event that you are planning and try to talk with their parent/carer to thank them for bringing their child to the club.

For church children

These children will have heard the Easter Day story many times and, as with the crucifixion, may cease to marvel at how Jesus could be resurrected. Pray that you can bring the story alive to them in a new way, enabling them to grow in their own faith. Encourage them to share what they know about the risen Jesus with the others in their Toolshed and then with their friends at school.

For children with other faiths

Reiterate for Muslim children that Jesus really was dead. Reiterate for Hindus and Buddhists that this is not reincarnation. Make sure that all the children understand the difference between this resurrection and the raising from the dead of the girl – she would die again, but Jesus will not. Muslim and Jewish children may be aware of other 'angel' stories so could help explain that angels are messengers. Emphasising the physicality of the resurrection – Jesus has a body that can be touched – may overcome misconceptions about 'souls'. Some children will be offended that the women worship Jesus and that he accepts it. Explain that this was their reaction to what God was doing.

For children with additional needs

For children who use signs (Makaton or British Sign Language) to communicate, try learning the signs for 'always' and 'forever'. You could even find the symbols for these words. This will help to reinforce the teaching.

It would be great if those children with additional needs and disabilities felt they could come to midweek and Sunday groups. Make it clear on follow-up fliers that your children's work is accessible by using the international symbols for accessibility.

Engineers' briefing

Spiritual preparation

Read Matthew 27:57–66; 28:1–10

Use the Bible version that the children are using. The burial of Jesus is not often read for we tend to concentrate on his death and then rush to his resurrection! What do people notice about Matthew's account that they have not seen before?

This session, children will hear that Jesus is alive and is with us at all times and in all places. Pray that as a team you will be conscious of him present with you throughout the club-time. Pray that each child will encounter the risen Christ and that they will know Jesus with them in the coming weeks and months. Conclude by giving thanks to God for all the evidence of his goodness that you have seen over the last week. Encourage everyone to pray short but urgent prayers.

Practical preparation

Talk through your programme together. Remind everyone of the key learning aims and who is doing what, ensuring that everyone knows their part in the day and has everything they need.

Set up the different areas of the club and make sure that everything is in place in plenty of time, so you are ready as the first children come from the registration area. Listen to any last-minute information or instructions from Boffin and Brainwave, or from the drama, music or refreshment teams.

Programme

Clocking in
10 minutes

Make sure the registration team is ready to greet and register the children.

By now everyone will be familiar with the routine. Children will be looking forward to meeting with others in their

What-you-need checklist
You will need:

- [ ] Registration: registration forms etc, badges, labels, pens, team lists
- [ ] The Mega Machine: a small hat, party hats, balloons, party poppers etc
- [ ] The Brainbox: for jokes, messages, questions and pictures
- [ ] Messy mechanics: ingredients for exploding volcano
- [ ] Technology: PA system, laptop, PowerPoints and projection/OHP and acetates, **Mega Makers!** DVD
- [ ] Mega words: a long strip of paper, ball of wool
- [ ] Toolsheds: materials for mini-machines and opening and closing activities; Bibles, *Inventor's Notebooks* or *Inventor's Sheets*, pictures of the five objects in the story
- [ ] Music: Innovation band or backing tracks
- [ ] Drama: costumes and props
- [ ] Activities: equipment for games and construction
- [ ] Boffin and Brainwave (presenters): running order, equipment for the Mega words, Learn and remember verse, praying for the wide world, quiz questions
- [ ] From the Maker's Manual: story script, props for the story
- [ ] Down tools: Drinks and biscuits or other refreshments

Toolshed group and hopefully will trust their leaders. They may be sad that this is the last day. Be ready to engage with the children, looking for opportunities to ask them what they are learning and discovering in the club, as well as talking with them about Jesus.

There may still be additions to the mini-machine. Alternatively, since wool is part of the Mega words, sit the children in a circle (which others can join as they arrive) and throw a ball of wool to a child on the other side of the circle. This child

PHASE 4

adds an additional word to the following sentence: 'My friends came to see me and they gave me a _____.' This child then holds onto the wool itself but throws the ball to another child who repeats the initial statement about the friend, the gift the first child has said and then the gift they received, and so on until you have a web. To make it more complicated for older children, their gift has to begin with the last letter of the previous gift.

Or you could make plaited friendship bracelets with thick wool if the children are up for it, or could complete the crosses started in the previous session.

The inventor's workshop
45 minutes all together

Once all the children are settled in the workshop, Boffin and Brainwave reintroduce themselves, setting the slapstick tone to the programme.

Stretch inventions

Elastic Eureka calls three leaders or older children to the front having primed them to invent a body position which they can hold in a frozen position for 15 seconds (or longer if children are able to sustain it) and which is physically possible for younger children. Since friendship is central to this session, they could invent positions which involve holding hands or hugging a friend(s). Play a stretch invention jingle while the children 'stretch'.

Mega Machine

Boffin reminds Brainwave of how they fell out last time and how angry Brainwave had been. Brainwave anxiously asks Boffin if he still loves him and is reassured that they are still friends. Boffin is very pleased with how the Mega Machine is working and thinks that the trialling period is over. But Brainwave wants to have just one more try. He throws a small hat into the machine and, after the usual noises and squeaks, the following burst out – party hats, plus balloons, blowouts and anything that reminds you of a party.

Boffin laughs and says that the Mega Machine must know that now is the time for celebrating. They lark around, while the Mega Machine makes various triumphant-style noises.

Messy mechanics
Exploding volcano

This will be done as a demonstration with a little help from volunteers. Test this out before the demonstration!

You will need:

- a large bowl
- 850 g of plain flour
- 320 g of salt
- 480 ml of water
- 4 tablespoons of cooking oil
- an empty half-litre plastic bottle
- a large oven dish
- 6 drops of washing-up liquid
- red food colouring
- 2 tablespoons of bicarbonate of soda
- vinegar
- towels to clear up the mess

Mix the flour, salt, some water and cooking oil together until it is smooth but not sloppy, varying the amount of water to obtain the right consistency. Put the plastic bottle in the oven dish and mould your mixture around it to form the volcano's cone. Unscrew the cap and pour in warm water almost to the top. Add a splash of red food colouring, six drops of washing-up liquid and two tablespoons of bicarbonate of soda. Gently start to pour vinegar into the bottle. The volcano will erupt with a satisfyingly realistic flow of bright red carbon dioxide foam 'lava'.

Comment on how it takes power for the lava to come out of the volcano and that Jesus used a different kind of power to rise from death.

Music makers

Reintroduce Innovation and sing the **Mega Makers!** theme song, along with any actions. Sing a song that you have already sung at **Mega Makers!** and maybe introduce a new one today.

From the Maker's Manual

Boffin reminds Brainwave of the party they had now that the Mega Machine is working properly. Brainwave is full of smiles! Boffin says that the story of Jesus dying was so sad but he came alive again and that is worth celebrating. Brainwave asks to hear the story again.

Storytelling options

Each day, there are three options suggested for telling the Bible story: you can use the same approach each time, mix and match how you tell the story, or combine two or more approaches. Choose which will be most helpful for your team, your children and the style of your club.

- The storyteller tells the story based on Matthew 28:1–s10 using their own words if possible (see page 7 for tips on how to do this). You can use the section headings and interactive ideas from the script (see option 3) as memory joggers and to vary your story presentation each time.
- Introduce today's episode from the **Mega Makers!** DVD. (If you are telling the story and using the DVD, tell the story first, then show the DVD so the children already have the outline of the events before seeing the episode.) In today's episode of the DVD we'll be back on location at all the places we've been this week – the Eden Project, the aquarium, Bug World and with the birds of prey. We'll be exploring how the precious world that God made needs us to work hard to look after it – to conserve nature for future generations. Gemma and Bob will explore these issues and find what we can do to help, and Bob will tell the wonderful story of how, after Jesus had died, he came back to life – meaning that God's love goes on forever and ever!
- Or the storyteller may prefer to follow the fully scripted retold Bible story for Day 5 on pages 74 and 75.

Storytelling method: Story bag
The storyteller needs to make sure they are familiar with the script and Matthew's version of the story so that they can tell the story fluently (in their own words), maintaining eye contact with the children.

You will need:
- A large bag or sack, decorated to look interesting. Inside are five objects that you need to tell the story. (Children love story bags and wait with anticipation to see what comes out next.)
- A toy shield
- A pair of ear muffs/plugs
- A pair of sunglasses
- A pair of running shoes
- A pair of men's open-toed sandals

(These could be wrapped up in shiny paper. Or you could display some images of these objects on PowerPoint)

Mega words

'FOR EVER AND EVER – friendship with Jesus'

Each day has a key phrase (which is in two parts, the 'enlarging words', and the subject of expansion). This will help children to remember what they have learnt and will keep leaders focused on the message they want children to learn.

At the end of a ball of wool, tie the phrase 'FOR EVER AND EVER – FRIENDSHIP WITH JESUS' printed on to a long piece of paper. Roll the paper up into a tight tube then wind wool around the 'tube' until the paper is covered and looks like a large ball of wool that will roll away from you – but not too far because the 'tube' needs to be discovered.

How do the children feel at the start of the summer holidays? Does it seem as though they have got weeks and weeks before they go back to school? Does that seem like for ever? Jesus went back to heaven but he said that he would never leave his friends but would be with them for ever and ever. That means he will be with us for ever and ever!

Begin to unwind the ball of wool so that it rolls away from you. Someone else may need to unwind it. The further away the ball goes from you the better, especially if it is almost out of sight. As it unrolls comment that maybe this ball of wool goes on for ever and ever! Eventually the Mega words are revealed. Show them to the children, who say the phrase three times.

Ask an engineer

Interview an older leader who has known Jesus as a friend for years and years. Ask them how old they were when they first realised that they were Jesus' friend and had become his follower. Comment that even though this leader has known Jesus for many years (which may seem a very long time to the children) it is not very long considering that Jesus died around 2,000 years ago. Now that is a long time! Ask this leader what it means for them practically to have Jesus as their friend, being careful to use language the children can understand.

Learn and remember

'I pray that you, together with all God's people, may have the power to understand how broad and long, how high and deep, is Christ's love.'

Ephesians 3:18 (GNB)

By now many of the children will know this verse. So read out verse 19 to them and ask them what they think the phrase 'filled with all that God is' means.

Explain that when someone becomes a follower of Jesus, the Holy Spirit (Jesus everywhere) comes to be with that person in a special way. It is like when you have had a delicious meal (but have not eaten so much that your tummy hurts). You are full up and feel satisfied and content. The more we know about God and actually know him, the more we experience his love for us and it is as though we have had a deeply satisfying meal. Deep inside us we are content, for God loves us and is with us. Of course, we also know that there is far more to discover about God and we are really keen to go on discovering more.

The Learn and remember song uses the phrase 'filled up with the fullness of God'.

Power drill
45 minutes in small groups

Down tools

Make sure children are comfortable as they settle for refreshments. As this is the last day and there is good news to share, you could provide special party food of some sort. As you eat and drink, say that you are going to go round the circle so that each person can share what has been the best bit about **Mega Makers!** and what one thing they have learnt about Jesus. Give them some suggestions if you think some children will find this a challenge.

Bible discovery
With older children (8–10s)

Begin by calling out the following words or phrases one by one and getting the children to react to them in some way: earthquake, object falling from the sky, big sound of huge rock being rolled along, super-bright light shining in your face.

If you told the story using objects in From the Maker's Manual, go through the five objects (showing pictures from the website or real objects) and ask the children to tell you the story, as a way of refreshing their memories. Then read Matthew 28:1–10 together from *Inventor's Notebook* on pages 38 and 39. If you have competent readers, ask if they would like to read the story, with one being the narrator and the others being the angel and Jesus. Ask the children what part(s) of the story they've never heard before. (It is likely that even children in the church will not be familiar with all the details so they will have something to say, as will children who are not usually in church.) Then talk about what part of the story the children think is the most surprising. Invite the children to fill in the boxes on page 41 to discover what Jesus first said when he met the women. What words can the children think of to describe how the women felt as the story unfolds? Get them to write these down on the lines on pages 40 and 41. Ask the children what they think the women did after Jesus told

PHASE 4

them to tell the others. Emphasise that this is such good news, everyone needs to hear it! Do the codebreaker on page 43 to discover what Jesus promised his disciples and talk about how this is a promise for us today, too. Look together at 'becoming a follower of Jesus' on page 44 and get the children to circle the statement that best describes where they are at. Encourage any child who wants to know more about following Jesus to talk with you or suggest who else they might like to talk with.

With younger children (5–8s)

Ask the children what good things have happened to them recently and who they wanted to tell the news to. If you told the story as suggested in From the Maker's Manual, go through the five objects (showing pictures or real objects) and ask the children to tell you the story, as a way of refreshing their memories. If not, read Matthew 28:1–10 using a child-friendly Bible or retell it with your own words. Using Inventor's Sheet 5, ask the children how the two women felt in each of the pictures.

Talk about how even though the angel was quite scary, he had good news for them. What was it?

Invite the children to work out which line of wool leads to the picture where Jesus meets the two women. What do the children think the women did after Jesus told them to tell the others?

Talk together about the people they could talk to about Jesus. Invite the children to write the name of this person in the speech bubble and encourage them to ask Jesus to give them the best words to say.

Encourage any child who wants to know more about following Jesus to talk with you or suggest who else they might like to talk with.

With all ages

How do you think you would respond if you saw an angel like the one described in the passage?

- Do you think you would have believed what the angel said?
- What did he point out that might have convinced you?

Power tool

The women were so happy that Jesus was alive and they had met him! Wow!

In the weeks and years to come these two women (and all Jesus' followers) were to discover that Jesus would be their friend for ever and ever. They would travel far and wide telling others that Jesus is alive.

Who could the children tell about Jesus? Ask them to think about this quietly and then pray for that person. You could pass a running shoe around the group (if you used the five objects in the version of the story above) as a symbol of telling others.

Explain that there are four suggestions for what a child can say to Jesus as they hold the shoe.

- They can name the person they are thinking of and pray a simple prayer such as: Jesus, help me to tell ___ that you are alive and want to be their friend. Amen.
- For children who may not know much about Jesus they can talk with Jesus along these lines: Jesus, I don't know much about you. Help me to get to know you. Amen.
- A child can pass the shoe onto the next child.
- A child may want to say something else to Jesus, so do encourage them to do so.

Make sure that you have a conversation with any child who prays the second option, to ask how you can help them to get to know Jesus better.

Construction

Choose a construction activity from pages 63 to 67. For extra craft ideas, see Ultimate Craft (SU 978 1 84427 364 5).

Games

Help the Mechanics shape up by choosing suitable games from pages 67 to 69. For more games ideas see Ultimate Games (SU 978 1 84427 365 2).

Back to the workshop
25 minutes

Brainbox

Edit the jokes, messages, pictures and questions in the Brainbox today. Marvel at any inventions that children have brought to show everyone else. If you are going to feature the Brainbox in the service on Sunday, encourage children to bring their final contributions.

Music makers

Innovation lead the children in a couple of lively songs.

Drama: Professor Ventor's Miracle Matter-Maker

Introduce the next episode of the comedy-drama, 'Professor Ventor's Miracle Matter-Maker'. Yesterday, the professor thought the Mechanical Miracle Matter-Maker was destroyed for good, but then ROBOT stepped in and became part of the machine. Today the professor, May, Saw, Claw and Bore think of ways they can spread the good news about this amazing super-invention.

Wide, wide world

The prayers for the world today follow the theme of Jesus being a friend for ever and ever. It is in school that children will have many opportunities to tell others about Jesus, so it is appropriate on the last day of the club to pray for the schools that the children attend. Draw a simple map of your locality with local schools clearly marked. Ask the children to go to a marked area/corner in the room for the school that they attend. Team members can lead the children in praying for their teachers, for new children, for any specific needs or things to thank God for. Parents or staff connected to the school could provide relevant information for the adults in each group and the children are likely to have lots of ideas. Conclude by praying that each child present will be able to share something about Jesus with their friends at school in the coming weeks.

Bench test

Divide the children into equal teams and devise a quiz which relates to all that has happened during **Mega Makers!** This can include funny events that happened unique to your club (show images on the screen if you have been making a photographic record), as well as facts from the stories, the Learn and remember verse and the Mega words. Use the key words to summarise the story and to reinforce what the children have learnt and discovered about Jesus. This is the final opportunity with many children to review the week.

Fusion finale

Round off Back to the workshop by asking several children to say in one sentence what one thing they will share when they get home. Children are used to doing this in school. Leaders can ask a similar question when the children are back in their Toolsheds. Conclude by thanking God for all the fun of the club and thanking all the team and other adults who have contributed.

Boffin reminds everyone about the collection routine, the service on Sunday and any other follow-up events planned.

Clocking off
10 minutes

Make sure that children have what they need to take home. Ask the children what one thing they are going to share about **Mega Makers!** when they get home.

Workshop clear-up
30 minutes

Once the children have gone, tidy up and if possible have a meal together as a celebration with time to enjoy each other's company. There may not have been a chance for lengthy conversations during the club. Encourage team members to feed back any comments they have about the club that will feed into the wider ministry to children and the next holiday club that you run. Ask for feedback immediately, before people forget. There is an evaluation sheet available online.

PHASE 4

mega makers!

PHASE 4

SUNDAY 2 THE FOLLOWERS OF JESUS

More & more

Key passage
Matthew 28:16-20

Key storylines
- Jesus has come alive again and over the next 40 days he appeared several times to his disciples. The angel at the tomb had told the women to instruct the disciples to meet Jesus back in Galilee, where it all began.
- At this meeting on a mountain Jesus gives them a challenge to go all over the world teaching others about him, so that they too could become followers of Jesus.

Key aims
- To hear about and reflect on the challenge Jesus gave (and gives) to those who follow him so that more and more people could become followers.
- To share with the rest of the church family what has been happening in the holiday club.
- To welcome any children and parents/ carers who have been part of the club but do not usually come to worship. The service therefore needs to bear some similarity to both the holiday club but also to a normal Sunday service.

For children with no church background
Children who have come all week still often find it a bit of a shock coming to church on Sunday. They may expect it to be the same as the holiday club, but no matter how hard we try, if it is a church service it will seem very different to them. Early in the service make sure familiar friends are involved and familiar activities included. Make it as much part of the holiday club as you can.

For church children
These children are used to church – so surprise them by how much like the holiday club it is. Make it the best service they have ever been to! Be sure to include as many of their favourite things from the holiday club as you can – songs, verses, the Mega Machine, as well as the Bible story about Jesus' challenge to his followers.

For children of other faiths
Encourage the children to invite their families to this service. Use the word 'families' rather than parents as many Asian families operate as a family unit which can be quite large. So don't be surprised if the whole family comes along (parents, siblings, aunties, grandpa etc). Have people of different ages ready to welcome them. Make sure they have seats, especially the adults. Think carefully about how to build on the relationships you have made with these children and their families. People need to be around to invite them to other appropriate events such as parents' and toddlers' group, old people's day club or family fun events.

For children with additional needs
Think about the family situations. Now that you have a good relationship with the child, how can you, as a church or as an individual, support the family in the future? This could be through babysitting, providing meals, washing, shopping or being a befriender in a regular children's group.

Service outline

What-you-need checklist

You will need:

- [ ] A box wrapped up in shiny paper containing up to 64 sweets, to be used in 'Setting the scene'

- [ ] A means of scoring in the quiz which increases in size, eg each team has a collection of shapes of people and for each correct answer they add another person to the 'group' until there is a crowd

- [ ] Copies of the Bible reading and two readers

- [ ] A flip chart and pens, an artist, sticky notes/small pieces of paper, pens/ pencils

- [ ] A long, long strip of paper on which are the words 'I will be with you for ever, and ever and ever......' with 'ever' repeated as many times as you can – at least 3 metres long

Suggested songs

Songs can be confessional since this is a service of Christian worship but be aware that visitors may not know the songs and may not want to sing words that they neither understand nor believe. Aim to sing as many of the songs from the club that you can.

- ⊚ Go tell it on the mountain
  Junior Praise 65
- ⊚ God is an awesome God
  Light for everyone CD, SU
- ⊚ Our God is a great big God
  Songs of Fellowship 2004
- ⊚ **Mega Makers!** theme song
- ⊚ *Learn and remember* verse song

Welcome

An all-age service provides the opportunity for some of the craft and activities from the holiday club to be displayed. Assemble a gallery of work in the entrance as people come in to the church, or in an area where you might serve refreshments. Ensure you have team members at the door to welcome holiday club children and their families

to the church, and show them where everything is. This will help people feel at ease as they enter a building they may not be familiar with. It may help the regular congregation if the welcome is done by someone who regularly leads services, while Boffin and Brainwave lead other parts. You will want to have the Mega Machine on display.

Begin with an appropriate well-known song or hymn. Follow this with some stretch inventions, which could repeat ones you have done during the club. Introduce the Mega Machine and, if your drama team are available, get them to perform the final sketch from the drama 'Professor Ventor's Mechanical Miracle Matter-Maker'. (See page 82 for the script.)

Set the scene

The leader announces that they have a treat inside a wrapped-up box which they want to share with someone. They choose one person who comes to the front as quickly as they can. (This all needs to be done briskly!) They explain to this person, in the hearing of everyone else, that they want others to share this so the leader and this person each call one person to the front, making four. The leader says that they need some more, so the four each invite one more, which makes eight. This is repeated until there are at the front as many as you can accommodate – 32 or 64! Share out the sweets, one for each person and then they sit down.

When Jesus started travelling around and telling others about God, he had just a few followers who travelled with him. (See if any children can remember their names and the story of Matthew's call.) But now after his death and new life, he wanted lots and lots more people to hear and be taught about him – one person telling another, who tells another and so the numbers grow, just like the crowd coming to share the treat grew. This is the story we are going to hear in this service.

Introductory activity

A quiz would help to review what the children have learnt over the holiday club as well as make the point that Jesus started out with a small group of

followers. Amend these questions as appropriate. Explain that some of the questions have several right answers.

- ⊚ What was the name of the tax collector who followed Jesus? (**Matthew**/Simon/Peter)
- ⊚ When did Matthew entertain Jesus for a meal? (breakfast, **dinner**, cup of hot chocolate)
- ⊚ What did Thomas Alva Edison invent in 1879? (**the light bulb** – a practical one that was commercially produced, but several other bulbs had been invented before this but not as effective.)
- ⊚ What did Jacob Fussell invent in 1850? (**mass-produced ice-cream**)
- ⊚ When Jesus got in the boat with his disciples, did he (talk with them/help steer the boat/**go to sleep**)?
- ⊚ What did his disciples think after Jesus had calmed the storm? (Fancy Jesus being my friend/**Jesus is amazing**/sad)
- ⊚ Why did a man come and kneel at Jesus' feet on Day 3? (**his daughter was dead**/he had bad knees/he was praying)
- ⊚ What happened to the man's daughter when Jesus went into the house? (**Jesus took her by the hand and she sat up**/the girl had disappeared/Jesus said they must wait for several hours before he could do anything)
- ⊚ What did the religious leaders think about Jesus? (They were not sure/ they liked listening to him/**they wanted to get rid of him**)
- ⊚ What did Jesus' friends think about Jesus? (all three are right – **they wanted to follow him/they were scared/they were not sure**)
- ⊚ What did the soldiers think about Jesus? (two are right – **it was just their job**/ they tried to rescue him/**they thought he was the Son of God**)
- ⊚ What did the crowd think of Jesus? (all three are right – **they didn't care/they thought he was a celebrity/one day they thought he was great, the next they wanted him dead**)
- ⊚ What four things happened when the women went to the tomb on Easter Day? (all four are right – **there was an earthquake, an angel came down to roll the stone away/the guards fell down as though dead/the women**

PHASE 4

mega makers!

PHASE 4

met Jesus as they left the tomb)

Conclude by seeing how many children can come to the front to say the Learn and remember verse. Display the words so that the rest of the congregation can read it. Ask the children to explain some of the truths about God that you have discovered from the verse. You could also sing the Learn and remember verse song if you have used it.

Bible reading

Two people will be needed to read Matthew 28:16–20. One person is the narrator while the second reads the words of Jesus.

Bible talk

Storytelling method: audience participation

Good news is worth sharing. Ask for suggestions of ways people can tell someone a piece of good news, eg phone, email, text, social networking, letter, personal conversation, visit someone, get on a bike/bus/train/plane/boat/horse. Write down the suggestions on a flip chart.

Jesus' followers had been told by Jesus to go to the people all over the world. Set the story in its context of time (after the cross and resurrection, reminding everyone of the last two days teaching in the club) and its geographical location (Galilee). They had to share the best news ever. But they lived 2,000 years ago. Run through the ways suggested above. Which of these ways could they use? (letter, personal conversation, visit someone, horse, boat)

But what exactly were they told to do? You could display the emboldened words on a Powerpoint.

- **Jesus said, 'Go and make followers of all people in the world'** – tell people and show them what it means to follow Jesus.
- **Jesus said, 'Baptise them in the name of the Father and the Son and the Holy Spirit'** – explain that baptism is a sign that someone wants to be washed clean from the wrong things they have done and is also a sign that

someone has become part of the crowd of Jesus' followers.

- **Jesus said, 'Teach them to obey everything that I have taught you'** – so what do you think are the things his *followers* had heard that Jesus said and that they had seen him do that they would want to tell someone about?

Using a flip chart, someone who is good at drawing cartoons or simple images, can illustrate each suggestion (in a *Pictionary* style – so much better than writing it down!) eg a heart for 'loves people', a hand stretched out to a child's hand, as Jesus did with the religious leader's daughter for 'makes people well/heals people', arrow downwards towards earth for 'comes from God', one stick figure following another for 'calls people to follow him'.

Give out small pieces of paper/sticky notes and ask people to write/draw the one thing Jesus has said or done which they would want to share with someone as good news, for these instructions from Jesus go on for ever and ever. They can repeat an image that has been written/drawn on the flip chart or think of something different. Stick these notes on an object associated with the holiday club such as the Mega Machine. (Don't put pressure on visitors to do this.)

- **Jesus said, 'I will be with you always, even until the end of this age.'** Jesus wanted his followers in the story to obey what he told them. He promised to be with them for ever. He wants us to follow him too and he promises to be with us, for ever and ever!

Wonder what would happen if you put a small piece of paper in the machine! Take a small piece on which is written, 'I will be with you for ever and ever.' Place it in the Mega Machine and out of it comes a long, long strip of paper on which is written 'I will be with you for ever, and ever and ever...' The strip unrolls but you do not get to the end of the 'for evers'. (Be sure that you know 'exactly how far the strip

will stretch from the Mega Machine.)

When you are at school, or work, or out with friends, or having a sleepover, or in hospital or feeling sad … Jesus promises to be with you.

Now that is all really good news! And it means that there will be people all over the world in their millions who over 20 centuries have been and are now following Jesus. You could refer to the crowd in the quiz and if you have Christians from other parts of the world worshipping with you draw attention to them, if appropriate.

Prayer

Lead several short prayers thanking God for the holiday club, ending by praying that each person will know that Jesus is with them, for ever.

Make it clear what anyone should do if they want to find out more about what it means to be a follower of Jesus. Also make sure that everyone knows what else is planned to maintain contact with the children who have come to the club who do not usually come, such as a Light Party or Saturday, half-term, Advent, or Christmas events for children and their families. Refreshments are an opportunity for leaders to meet up with family members.

RESOURCE BANK

Mega toolkit

Here in the Toolkit you'll find many of the resources you need for **Mega Makers!**: the scripts for telling the Bible story; craft and game ideas including templates; the theme song and *Learn and remember* verse song; the Bible discovery notes and 'Professor Ventor's Miracle Matter-Maker' drama. You can photocopy those pages marked 'Photocopiable'. For all other resources go to www.scriptureunion.org.uk/megamakers.

CONSTRUCTION

In this section you'll find five construction projects that don't involve something the children take home but look at solving problems with simple materials, *and* five constructions related to the Bible theme for each day – these will result in a take-home item. There are also a number of extra ideas.

Clever inventions!

These five construction projects look at solving problems with simple materials. The children will probably not end up with something that they can take home with them, but the process of solving the problem will create an environment where you can strengthen relationships, chat about the day's teaching and have fun together. It might be useful for each Toolshed leader to have a strong pair of scissors, for their use only, just in case child-safe scissors are not sufficient.

Invention 1
Keeping an egg safe

What you need
- A variety of junk, such as egg boxes, cardboard, paper, bubble wrap, yogurt pots, kitchen roll
- Child-safe scissors and sticky tape
- An egg per Toolshed (preferably raw, but if you're concerned about the mess, then hard-boil the eggs the night before the session)
- Plastic sheeting (optional)

What you do
Before the session, find a high point in your meeting space from where you can drop the eggs in their protective casings. Make sure you risk assess how you will get up there. Spread some plastic sheeting over the 'drop-zone' if you are concerned about egg leakage!

Share out the junk materials and give each Toolshed leader an egg. Instruct the Mechanics that they have to make a protective casing for their egg that will stop it from breaking when you drop it from a high height. Show them the point from which you'll drop the eggs and make a show of how high it is!

Toolshed leaders should help their groups to do a little bit of planning before they start. Then they should let the children create the best casing for their egg. Everyone will have to work together to finish the project.

When everyone is ready, take the eggs to your high point and drop them off in turn. If you're using points, score each effort but ensure you make positive comments about every attempt!

Invention 2
Sending a message

What you need

- Balloons, drinking straws, string
- Paper, card, small boxes and any spare junk (see invention 1)
- Pens
- Child-safe scissors and sticky tape

What you do

Tell the children that they have to transport a message from one side of your meeting space to the other. Give out the materials you have to each of the Toolsheds. Toolshed leaders and assistants should help the children think through how they might do it. One way is to thread a long piece of string through a piece of drinking straw. Tie the string across your meeting space, then tape a balloon to the straw. Make some kind of device to hold a message (could be a box or loop of paper) and fix that to the straw. When you have written your message and secured it to the straw, blow the balloon up and let go. The balloon should travel along the string, taking the message to the other side of the room.

You might want to give the children the chance to experiment with paper aeroplanes. There are plenty of different methods on the internet. Print a few off and let the children decide which method is the best. How far can they send their messages?.

Alternatively, let the children use their imaginations with what you have provided!

If you're awarding points, give points for the furthest travelled, but also for the most stylish or graceful travel, the most ingenious invention and the most unlikely success!

Invention 3
Tower building

What you need

- Marshmallows
- Spaghetti, craft straws or drinking straws
- Child-safe scissors

What you do

Give each Toolshed a packet of marshmallows and some spaghetti or straws. (If you don't want to waste any food, you could use polystyrene or organic packing pellets, though Toolshed leaders may need to help children push the straws in. If using packing pellets you may need to weigh down the base of the towers so they don't topple over.) Challenge them to build the tallest tower they can with the materials you have provided.

Allow everyone to experiment, and make sure you have extra supplies of all the materials in case of sudden and irreparable collapse!

At the end of your time, measure the tallest tower. How did that Toolshed manage to build such a tall structure? Again, if you're awarding points, award them for height, but also for appearance, perseverance and precariousness!

Invention 4
Catapult

What you need

- Elastic bands, shirring elastic or other stretchy materials
- Small sticks such as garden dowelling or bamboo skewers (make sure you cut any sharp ends off)
- Other junk modelling materials (see invention 1)
- Screwed-up balls of paper
- Child-safe scissors and sticky tape

What you do

Challenge the Toolsheds to fling a screwed-up ball of paper as far as they can, using the materials you have provided. There are a variety of ways they can do this – by making a slingshot, a catapult or even a trebuchet! You might wish to provide some plans or examples gathered from the internet to help groups.

Give plenty of time for each group to come up with and create their idea. You might need to give younger groups a bit more help.

When everyone is finished, try the inventions out and see who can fire the paper the furthest. If you're awarding points, consider giving points for the most graceful, the most inventive and the best failure!

Invention 5
Blazing a trail(er)!

What you need

- Small boxes such as cereal boxes or shoeboxes
- Other junk (see invention 1)
- Small sticks such as garden dowelling or bamboo skewers (make sure you cut any sharp ends off)
- Scissors, glue and string
- Remote-controlled car
- Small plastic balls (such as ball-pit balls)
- Felt-tip pens

What you do

Before the session, set out a route around your space, for a remote-controlled car to tow a trailer around.

Challenge the children to create a trailer that can be fixed to a remote-controlled car. Say that you're going to see how many balls each trailer can carry around the course. Each Toolshed should construct a trailer that can carry some plastic balls. It also needs to have a way to connect the trailer to the car. Give the children some time to decide how they will make the trailer, then Toolshed leaders should help the children to make it

When everyone is finished, connect each of the trailers up to the car, fill it with as many plastic balls as possible and tow the trailer round the course. As with the other activities, award points for other things, as well as how many balls each can carry.

Extra ideas

If you have the facilities to try something a bit more advanced that requires a little more equipment, try out some of these activities.

Electric circuit building

Physics sets are widely available and many of these include electric circuit activities. Challenge the groups to create circuits and discover together how the power flows through the wires. This would be a good activity to do on Day 2 or 3, when the club focuses on Jesus' power.

Magnets

Magnets are also a good thing to experiment with when talking about power. As with physics and circuit sets, there are plenty of magnet kits on the market. Use some of the experiments that come with the kits to explore a little bit about the power of magnets. As you discover things together, chat about what the children think about Jesus' power.

Construction sets such as LEGO® Technic or Meccano®

If you have access to construction sets, then these would be good to use in your construction time. Makes such as LEGO®, LEGO® Technic or Meccano® are widely available, as are magnetic stick and ball sets such as Geomag and Magnetix. (There may be people in your church who can lend kits to you.) Gather lots of different sets together (include makes that are suitable for younger children as well as Key Stage 2). Challenge the Toolsheds to follow the instructions for their particular kit, or give them the chance to create something new! If the sets are particularly complex, then this could run over more than one session.

Getting dads involved! (And mums!)

If you have parents who are good with wood, inventive and willing to give up some time, you could get them involved and try some more ambitious inventions, such as go-karts. Make sure you risk assess anything you choose to do, particularly if you're using tools such as saws or hammers. However, with proper supervision, children will have an amazing time creating something more substantial!

Construction that links to the story

Day 1
Bread-making

What you need
- The ingredients for your chosen bread recipe
- Clean-up and cover-up equipment
- Baking facilities and adults to operate them

What you do
Before the session, decide how you are going to make bread. There are a variety of options:
- You can buy ready-to-use bread mix. This only needs to be mixed with water and doesn't require long to prove. You will still need to knead this for a short time, but the children will enjoy doing that!
- There are several soda bread recipes available on the internet. Soda bread doesn't use yeast, but relies on bicarbonate of soda reacting with the cultures in buttermilk to make it rise. It doesn't need much kneading or any proving, so is ideal for making in a short space of time. It will require measuring and mixing, so you can enjoy doing that together!
- Pizza dough is a good alternative to bread. It can be bought in ready-to-mix packs, or made from scratch (there are plenty of recipes available on the web). It requires some kneading but no proving, so is suitable for a holiday club context!

As you make your chosen bread, chat together about what the children like to eat and what kind of food they like to have at parties or when people come to visit.

Day 2
Paper boats

What you need
- Sheets of A4 paper (you might want each child in a Toolshed to have a different colour, so you can tell them apart)

PHASE 5

- Instructions for each group on making a paper boat (see resource page 91)
- Child-safe scissors and sticky tape
- Crayons
- A large tank filled with water (optional)

What you do

Show the children in your group how to make a paper boat using resource page 91. If you have time, you could also show them one or two others ways of making a paper boat (available on the internet).

As you work to create your paper boats, chat about the story you heard today. What do they think about what Jesus did? Encourage the children to decorate their boats (with crayons, so that the colour won't run in the water). Display the boats for everyone to see, before taking them home.

If you have the facilities, try the boats out in a large tank full of water. Decide together which boat might sail the best. If your children are happy to let you, you could make waves in the water to watch the boats go up and down. How might the disciples have felt in a boat that was going up and down like the ones in the tank?

Day 3
Pretty paper blankets

What you need
- Different coloured A4 paper
- Different coloured strips of paper (cut widthways from A4 paper)
- Child-safe scissors and sticky tape
- Felt-tip pens and/or crayons

What you do

Give the children a sheet of A4 paper in the colour of their choice. Show them how to fold this paper in half widthways, then cut slits in the paper from the fold to about 1 cm from the edge. When the children open the paper out, they should have slits that run the length of the paper (but that don't reach the edge). If the children want to, they can decorate their paper before they cut the slits. This will give a different pattern later.

Spread out the strips of paper and let the children choose the colours they'd like to use. Weave these strips in between the slits you have just cut in the sheet of paper. Encourage the children to alternate colours or use a different colour for each strip. Once all the strips are in place, you might want to secure the ends with some sticky tape. There are some photographs on the **Mega Makers!** website to help you.

As you work, talk about how the girl in the story was sick in bed. Say how colourful things

sometimes cheer you up when you're not well. Make sure your discussion goes onto the fact that the girl died, and Jesus brought her back to life! What do the children think about that?

Day 4
Love letter from God

What you need
- A4 sheets of card (any bright colour, not too dark)
- Red pieces of paper
- Two heart templates (see **Mega Makers!** website)
- Coloured thread or thin ribbon
- Felt-tip pens

What you do

Let the children choose a piece of card. Show them how to fold it in half across the middle to create a greetings card that is A5 in size. Using the larger of the two heart templates, draw a heart shape on the front of the card and cut it out, so that you have a heart-shaped hole on the front of the card.

Then, draw round the smaller heart template on a piece of red paper and cut that out. Help the children make a small hole in the top of the red heart, and a small hole at the top of the heart-shaped hole in the greetings card. Tie a small length of thread or ribbon through the top of the red heart. Then tie the other end of this thread through the hole at the top of the heart on the card. Make the thread short enough so that the red heart hangs freely in the heart-shaped hole in the greetings card. There are some photographs on the **Mega Makers!** website to help you.

Using the felt-tip pens, write 'For you' on the front of the card. Chat together about the fact that this card is a card from God saying how much he loves them. Thinking about today's story, what do they think God would write in the card? If possible, let the children write what they think. If they are struggling, give them a couple of options about what to write. Try something like:

'I love you so much and I want to be your friend!'

Day 5
Easter garden

What you need
- Corner yogurt pots
- Sterile compost
- Small clean round pebbles (one per child)
- Other small clean stones or gravel
- Moss, cress, herbs or other small plants
- Small strips of white cloth

What you do

You will need to start collecting corner yogurt pots a few months before the club starts. Ask your church (or your local primary school, if you have a good relationship with them) to wash them out and save them for you. You might want to remove any stickers on the sides of the pots before you use them.

Give everyone a corner yogurt pot. Help each child bend the pot so that the smaller corner is standing up, at 90° to the larger corner. Fill the larger corner with compost. The larger corner forms the garden and the smaller, upright corner represents the tomb where Jesus was buried.

Spread out the garden materials you have in front of the children, and let them plant whatever they like in their garden. They can also use the small stones to decorate the garden corner. Give each child a small strip of cloth and help them to fold it up and place it inside the smaller corner. Finally give each child a round pebble to place upright to one side of the tomb, as if it has been rolled back.

During this construction time, chat about the story. As you place the cloth in the tomb, talk about how Jesus wasn't there when the women came to see him. How might they have felt? What do they think about Jesus not staying dead, but coming back to life?

GAMES

Scrapyard

What you need

- Bamboo canes (or similar)
- String
- Magnets or large hooks
- Various bits of machinery (cogs, large screws, large washers, brackets etc) or 'junk' machinery (made of boxes, plastic pots etc and painted to look like parts of a machine) with loops attached
- Masking tape

What you do

Before the session, make some 'crane arms' (enough for one per team). Tie a length of string to the end of a garden cane and fix either a magnet or hook to the end of the string. If you are using real bolts and cogs etc, then make sure the magnet is strong enough to pick them up. If you're using 'junk' machinery, ensure that all the pieces have a loop on them large enough for the hook on the end of the string to be able to pick them up.

Mark off an area in your meeting place and spread your 'machine parts' out in that area. (You could use a large paddling pool or just mark out an area with masking tape.) Station the Toolsheds around the area and give each one a crane arm. Challenge the teams to gather as many machine parts as they can in a set time. Tell them that, after one person has hooked a machine part, they should pass the crane arm onto another in their team. (You'll need to have enough machine parts to ensure that you don't run out before the end of your time limit!)

At the end of the time, count up how many parts each Toolshed has collected. You could attach different numbers to each of the parts, and use those to award scores, rather than just counting the number of machine parts collected.

Lego relay

What you need

- Several sets of the same simple Lego model (or other construction toy)

What you do

Place the pieces of the simple model at one end of your space, and line the Toolsheds up at the other end. Show the Toolsheds a completed version of the model and say they have to make that model piece by piece. On the word 'Go!' each player should, in turn, run to the pieces of model, collect one of the pieces and bring it back to their team. Then they should try to construct the model – the first team to do so is the winner.

Patent protection!

What you need

- Two large (but portable) junk inventions (tape two large boxes together and decorate them to look like a machine)
- Two different colours of wool
- A large playing space, with two home bases far apart from each other

What you do

Before the session, prepare your two inventions and cut lots of lengths of wool (they should be long enough to be tied loosely around a child's wrist). Decide on how large your playing area is going to be and risk assess the whole game. The two bases should be in completely different parts of your building.

Split the children into two teams and appoint a couple of leaders to lead each team. Give the team leaders a different colour of wool and an invention to protect. Explain that each team has to protect their own invention while trying to steal the other team's invention. Instruct the leaders to give each person in their team a length of wool to loosely tie round their wrist. If, when they are trying to steal the opposition's invention, they are caught by someone on the other team, they have to give up their wool, and return to their own home base for another piece. Make sure everyone knows the playing area.

Send everyone to their home bases and start the game. Have neutral leaders positioned at any hazards you have in your building to ensure safety, and also to block any doors that the children shouldn't go through. These neutrals should also referee the rules!

At the end of the game, count up how many times a team captured their opponent's invention, as well as how many pieces of the opposition's wool they collected.

This game is chaotic, but great fun. Play for as long as the children are enjoying it (this may be long after the game has ceased to make sense!).

Mind that machine
What you need
- An obstacle course, where all the obstacles look like crazy inventions
- Stopwatch (optional)

What you do
Before the session, create an obstacle course and make the obstacles look like machines and inventions. This may seem a lot of effort, but will look amazing when you've finished, and create some great memories for the children. Make sure you risk assess your course before the children tackle it!

Challenge the Toolsheds to complete the obstacle course. You could do this as a relay or ask the whole Toolshed to go together. If you're awarding points, give some to the quickest team, but also to the team who did it knocking the fewest obstacles over or who completed the course with the most style!

Battleship inventions
What you need
- Masking tape
- A large screen or room divider
- Large sheets of paper (lining paper is ideal)
- Marker pens
- Two sets of five junk model inventions (each invention a different size)
- Lots of red and blue paper circles

What you do
This game will take a while to set up, but is worth doing for the experience the children will have. It is essentially a giant version of battleships. In your playing space, place your large screen or room divider across the centre of the room. On the floor on either side of the screen, mark out a grid of squares, six squares by six. Also write 1 to 6 down one side of the grid and A to F along the bottom. Draw out the same size grid twice on the large sheets of paper and hang those on either side of the screen/divider.

Make your two sets of inventions. Make one invention of the set the same size as one square, one invention two squares long, one three squares long, one four and one five squares long.

Position one Toolshed on either side of the screen and challenge them to place their inventions on the grid on the floor in front of them. In turn, each team names a square (eg F2 or B6). Their opponents have to say whether that square has an invention on it (or part of an invention) or is empty. The first team put a red circle on the corresponding square on the paper grid facing them if they have found part of an invention or a blue circle if that square is empty. The game continues until one team has found all the locations of all their opponent's inventions.

Go-go-gadgets!
What you need
- Parachute

What you do
Before the session, think of five inventions that the children will know. For example, you might choose an iPod, a mobile phone, a vacuum cleaner, a microwave and a light bulb. Spread out the parachute and ask the children to find a place around the edge. Go round and give each child one of the names of the inventions you have chosen.

Ask the children to pick up their edge of the parachute and practise lifting it up high and pulling it down again. After the children have got the hang of this, lift up the parachute together and shout out an invention: 'Vacuum cleaner!' All the children who were given the name 'Vacuum cleaner' have to run under the parachute and out the other side, before everyone else brings the parachute down again.

Keep playing, shouting out different inventions. Every so often shout 'Go-go-gadgets!' All the children should then run under the parachute to the other side. (Make sure you have enough adults spread around the edge of the chute to keep it from flying away when all the children let go!)

Target practice

What you need

- Any toy which can fire something a short distance (eg Nerf gun, foam disk shooter or even water pistol!)
- A large target (one with rings, where the outer ring is marked '2', the next '4', then '6' and '8' and the bullseye '10')

What you do

Position the target at one end of your playing space, and line the children up at an appropriate distance from it. Give the team your chosen toy and encourage them to shoot their missiles at the target. Let each child have three goes at hitting the target. When everyone has finished, add up how many points the team has scored. (As your toy is unlikely to make a mark on the target, have a leader whose job it is to see where the missile lands, while not getting hit themselves!)

You may need to give the children a practice before you start counting, so that they can work out where to aim! You could have two teams competing against each other, or have all the Toolsheds playing at once, depending on how many toys and targets you have. You could also compare which toys are the most accurate!

Mechanical board games

What you need

- A selection of children's games which involve whacky machines or inventions as part of the play, such as Mouse Trap, Buckaroo, Pop-up Pirate or Operation – make sure you have games suitable for all the ages in your club

What you do

This is ideal if you have a small amount of space or want a game which doesn't involve much running around or preparation. Before the session, gather together some children's games that involve some mechanical component. It's likely that people in your congregation will have some of these; otherwise a trip to your local charity shops might yield some great games for little money!

Set the games up and let the children choose which ones they want to play. Make sure Toolshed leaders get involved too, as games like these are ideal times to chat and build relationships while you play.

Water tower

What you need

- Outdoor space (or a large room with plenty of waterproof tarpaulins)
- A piece of drainpipe (about 5 feet or 1.5 m long) per Toolshed, with holes drilled up and down its length (these need to be small enough for children to cover them with their fingers) and one end blocked up
- A hosepipe and water supply or large jug of water

What you do

Arrange the children in a circle and place the drainpipe upright in the middle, with the blocked up end at the bottom. Start pouring water into the top of the drainpipe. As the water builds up in the pipe, it will start coming out of the holes you drilled. The children have to put their fingers over the holes. As the pipe fills they will have to cover more and more of the holes, and undoubtedly will get wet! At the end of a set time, measure how high up the pipe the water has got.

(You could do this one Toolshed at a time, meaning you only have to make one holey drainpipe!)

Robot fountain

What you need

- Outdoor space (or a large room with plenty of waterproof tarpaulins)
- A garden hose, connected to a water source
- A blindfold

What you do

Ask the children to stand in a circle (it might be helpful to mark a circle on the floor of your playing area). A blindfolded leader (the robot) stands in the middle of the circle with the hose. When the hose is turned on, the robot should try to splash the children around them, and the children should try to avoid getting wet. You could make it more difficult by saying that the children have to stay inside the circle (this will avoid the easy solution of just running out of range of the hose!).

Once the children are confident with the game, let them take turns at being the robot in the middle of the circle. You will need some leaders either standing by or taking part in the game to make sure it doesn't get out of hand!

(This game is adapted from one on the NHS Change4Life website – for more games ideas, go to www.nhs.uk/change4life/pages/fun-generator.aspx)

PHASE 5

mega makers! PHASE 5

FROM THE MAKER'S MANUAL:
BIBLE STORY SCRIPTS

Day 1

Set the scene

Jesus lived in a town called Capernaum which was on Lake Galilee. The sun often shone on the water there and you could catch a tasty fish or two. (*Hurray!*)

But this town was in an area ruled by a king called Herod Antipas. (*Boo!*)

Herod Antipas was big friends with the Romans who occupied the land where Jesus lived. (*Boo!*)

The Romans occupied several other regions around there too. (*Boo!*)

The town, Capernaum was on the border with several regions and on Lake Galilee. Food, tools, building materials, wood, cloth, goats, sheep, wine, equipment, (all that sort of thing), would come across the lake, or down the road across the border from one of these regions. That meant nice houses, warm clothes and good things to eat. (*Hurray!*)

But every time a boat-load or a donkey-load of stuff arrived in Capernaum from across the lake or over the border, tax collectors would demand money to be paid before the stuff could move on to wherever it was going. And these collectors would almost always ask for more money than they should do, so they just got richer and richer. (*Boo!*)

Some of this money they gave to Herod Antipas, the king (*Boo!*) and some of the money they gave to the Romans (*Boo!*) and some of this money they kept for themselves. (*Boo!*)

Ask how many children have been to another country. What do they know about duty free goods and customs and being searched for security reasons?

Introduce Matthew

Now let's hear about one of these tax collectors whose name was Matthew.

He was rich.

He lived in a big house.

He worked with other tax collectors.

He was unpopular.

Not many ordinary people liked him because they suspected that he cheated them whenever he charged them taxes for the food, tools, building materials, wood, cloth, goats, sheep, wine,

equipment, (all that sort of thing) that they brought into Capernaum on a donkey or in their boat from across the lake. (*Boo!*)

Jesus sees Matthew

One day Jesus came walking in the town. As far as we know on this occasion, he wasn't transporting food, tools, building materials, wood, cloth, goats, sheep, wine, equipment, (all that sort of thing), although sometimes he must have done. *Anyone know what Jesus' job was and what he might have been used to moving from Capernaum to other towns in the region, over the border and across the lake…?*

Jesus caught sight of Matthew, this unpopular tax collector. (*Boo!*)

Matthew was getting on with his job, collecting taxes and money from people.

The invitation

Jesus simply went up to Matthew and said to him, 'Come with me!'

Unlike most other people Jesus didn't say Boo! to Matthew. Instead he actually wanted Matthew to become one of his followers. Amazing! It was as though he had given Matthew an invitation to follow him, to come to his party! *Ask a child to open the envelope with Jesus' invitation to Matthew. Show the children.*

What do you think Matthew did? He got up and went with Jesus. Matthew was so pleased. He had never thought that someone like Jesus would want him for a friend! (*Hurray!*)

The party

Later that day, Matthew decided he was going to throw a party himself and he was going to invite Jesus to be his chief guest. *The storyteller puts on the fascinator or bow tie as befits a party-goer. (Hurray!) Invite a child to open the envelope with Matthew's invitation to Jesus and read it out.*

What do you think Jesus did? Some people would expect Jesus to refuse an invitation to a party at Matthew's house. You see Matthew didn't have ordinary, respectable people as friends. His friends were the people no one else liked. They needed to stick together…the cheats and the bullies and the poor and the people who got in trouble – that sort of person.

Well, Jesus went to the party. He'd got all the time in the world for people like this. And they had such a lot of fun and ate lots of good food and Jesus talked and told them some great stories and helped them to find out more about God. And they realised how much he loved them. And he gave each of them an invitation to follow him. *(Hurray!) Take out the pile of folded invitations and ask two children to unfold the pile. Ask another child to read what the invitation says. Note everyone gets the same invitation!*

Accepting the invitation

Jesus had already invited some fishermen to follow him. And they had accepted.

Now he had invited Matthew to follow him and Matthew accepted.

Over the next few months Jesus was going to invite lots of other people to come and follow him.

Some people decided right from the start that they didn't want to follow Jesus.

Some people followed him for a while and then got fed up or wanted to do something else.

Some people decided they were going to follow Jesus for the rest of their lives. Matthew was one of these and he became one of Jesus' special followers. And over the weeks and months Matthew put behind him for ever his life of collecting taxes dishonestly. *(Hurray!)*

Jesus invites all of us to come with him, whether we are loud or quiet, with lots of friends or with not many friends. *Point to the long pile of invitations.* The invitation is for everyone! Over **Mega Makers!** you will find out more about what it means to come with Jesus and realise how much he loves you. His invitation just reaches more and more people. It gets wider and wider!

Day 2

Introduce idea of 'following'

Comment on how Brainwave has been trying to follow Boffin and has got in the way. We can follow someone in lots of different ways. We can walk in their footsteps. We can make movements like they do, for example, speak like they do, sniff like they do, move our hands like they do, celebrate scoring a goal in football like _____. *(Give some examples of people known to the children.)* Or we can aim to actually become like them in the way that we think, make decisions or relate to other people. That sort of 'following someone' is much more challenging.

Jesus gets in boat

One day Jesus got into the fishing boat which some of his disciples owned. They were fishermen and knew all about boats and fishing. The boat was probably just over 8 metres long, 2 metres wide and

only 1.25 metres deep, so not very **deep** at all. *(Leader who is Jesus gets into the 'boat' outline.)*

Disciples get in boat

Introduce Jesus' disciples, saying that there were probably more than three who were around at this time, but these three represent all the others – and we don't know if Matthew (from yesterday) was included. (Ask the children if he was a fisherman? What was he?) These disciples followed Jesus and got into the boat with him. *(Disciples get in boat and begin to pull up an imaginary mast and sail, get some oars working and lay out their nets. The storyteller could ask them what they are doing. Jesus just sits and waits.)* Comment that following Jesus sometimes meant that the disciples got on with everyday life and what they were good at but knew that Jesus was with them.

The storm starts

(Disciples push out the boat from the seashore and do a bit of rowing and rock backwards and forwards in unison. They may get that wrong so the storyteller has to help them synchronise their movements. Jesus yawns and lies down with his head on a bit of equipment. He goes to sleep. But then the disciples' movements become more 'violent', they begin to look worried, as the wind gets up. All the time the storyteller comments on their actions.)

The storm gets worse

Explain that Lake Galilee was surrounded by hills and sometimes a terrifyingly fierce storm could come from nowhere. These fishermen knew all about fierce storms but this one beat them all. They were scared. They pulled down the mast. But the worst problem was that as the boat was not deep (how deep was it?), the water from the lake began to splash over the side. The water in the boat got more and more, while the side of the boat sank deeper and deeper into the lake. *(Disciples bail out the water with their hands.)* And all this time Jesus slept. Is this what following Jesus is all about? they thought. Jesus is with you but he leaves you to drown?

Wake up! Calm down!

In desperation they woke Jesus up. *(Energetic shaking of Jesus who immediately stands up.)* 'What are you afraid of?' Jesus said to them. 'Do you not trust me? How shallow is your faith? You need to let your faith get **deeper and deeper**.' Then Jesus called out to the wind and the waves. 'Be quiet! Calm down!' *(The Jesus actor could shout this out, which would be a surprise.)* And everything went immediately quiet. *(Disciples jerk to stillness. Then they stare at Jesus and at each other, open-mouthed.)* Stunned,

PHOTOCOPIABLE PAGE

PHASE 5

the disciples asked, 'How come Jesus can do this? Is he just an ordinary man, or someone with extraordinary powers, or is he God himself? Even the wind and the waves obey him.'

The challenge to follow

Following Jesus means making sure you know Jesus is with you in the ordinary times in life, like going to school, going to bed, playing with friends. But also when something goes wrong, you know that Jesus is there; you know he can be trusted to make a difference. (*Jesus gets out of the boat, winds up the rope while the disciples sit stunned and as Jesus slowly walks away they jump up and run to walk with him.*) It is all about your faith and trust in Jesus getting **deeper and deeper** the more you know him and are with him. That is what the disciples discovered in this story.

Day 3

1 JESUS SITS DOWN
Jesus was sitting down. (*Leader 1 sits down stiffly and slowly.*) Jesus often sat down to talk with people and to tell them stories and to explain to them what God was like and how much he loves and cares for the world he had made.

2 FATHER KNEELS DOWN
Suddenly a man came and stood directly in front of Jesus and went down on his knees. (*Leader 2 goes down on both knees and bows his head. He can wipe his eyes with a handkerchief.*) Explain who he is: a leader at the synagogue, an important person. He might have heard negative things said about Jesus by some of the religious leaders or he might have only heard good things about Jesus' miracles.

3 FATHER HOLDS OUT HANDS, PLEADINGLY
'My daughter has just died,' he said, just like that. 'But come to our house. Lay your hand on her and she will live.' (*Leader 2 holds his hands out towards Jesus.*)

4 JESUS WALKS WITH FATHER
Jesus got up and went with the father to the father's house. (*Leader 1 gets up and starts walking away.*)

5 JESUS KNOCKS ON DOOR
Jesus went into the house with the father to find the dead girl. (*Leader 1 walks up to an imaginary door and knocks on it.*)

6 JESUS SHOOS MUSICIANS AWAY
In those days as soon as someone had died, professional musicians were called in to make lots of noise and announce to everyone that there has been a death in the house so there was lots of crying and sadness. These musicians had already been called, for the girl had been dead some time by now. Jesus shooed them away from the door. (*Leader 1 shoos people away.*) But they laughed at him loudly.

7 JESUS TAKES GIRL'S HAND
But Jesus would not be put off. He said a most surprising thing, 'Your daughter is not dead, only sleeping.' Then he went into the girl's room. She really was dead but Jesus took hold of her hand. (*Leader 1 bends over to take the girl's hand*)

8 GIRL GETS UP
Just like that, the girl sat up. (*Leader 3 gets up slowly from a lying position.*) She is alive!

So how did this all happen? Did Jesus have so much power in his arm that he could pull the girl to life? (NO!)

Jesus' power

What sort of power did he have to make someone come alive again? It was not that he had strong arms or could force people to do things. It was a bit more like the power of electricity – you cannot see electricity but you know it is powerful to make electrical equipment work, to burn lights, to light a whole city! Jesus' power came from within himself and as he was God, his power was God's power, with power to create the world, calm a storm and bring a girl back to life. He just touched her. Her body was the same, just as it was before she died, but she was well and she was breathing. (She did die eventually although we don't know when. Her death had just been postponed.)

The news spreads

And what happened to the man and his daughter? Did they become followers of Jesus? The father had had such deep trust in Jesus and his power. He had seen an extraordinary thing happen in his home! We don't know what happened but we do know that news about Jesus spread all over that part of the country. Everyone was talking about him. If Jesus could bring someone alive again he could do anything – and of course, these people did not know that God's power would bring Jesus himself alive again a couple of years later. But unlike the girl in our story, his new body could do more things than his old body; his new body was one which would never die.

Day 4

Summary of Jesus' life so far

Explain that Jesus had been sharing with people about how much God loves them. He had been telling great stories to help people understand this. He had made sick people well, calmed a storm and even made dead people come alive again – as we have already heard. But his enemies did not like what he said or did. They hated him and the more he said and did, the more they hated him. They wanted to get rid of him. They wanted him dead.

Gethsemane

Jesus knew this. He knew that he was going to die. On the Thursday evening, the day before he died, he had a special meal with his friends and then they went out to a vineyard.

He was so very troubled and sad. He began to talk with God his Father (probably out loud), kneeling with his face to the ground, begging God to save him from having to die. Deeply sad and very afraid he accepted that he had to die. He loved and trusted God his Father and knew that his Father loved him. So he was prepared to do what his Father wanted.

He turned to his three closest friends (Peter, James and John) for comfort but they had fallen asleep. They wanted to help Jesus, but just could not keep awake. Three times he talked with God his Father and three times his friends fell asleep. Soon after that, at the dead of night, his enemies arrested him.

Jesus' enemies

Jesus had three types of enemies:

- the religious leaders who didn't like what Jesus said about God or what he did.
- the Roman authorities who wanted to get rid of anyone who might cause trouble – they wanted to keep the peace
- some people Jesus had met who deep down were not really interested in knowing God and resented what Jesus said and did.

Religious leaders

It was the religious leaders who arranged for his arrest. (*Remove the RELIGIOUS LEADERS cloth.*) They hated him so much. They hated what he said about God and worse, that he said he was God himself! How dare he say something like that! After Jesus' arrest, they sent him to their own court where he was judged. It was a very unfair trial. (*Turn the chair/person round to show the back.*)

Jesus' friends

Jesus' friends loved Jesus and they knew that he loved them. (*Remove the JESUS' FRIENDS cloth.*) They did not understand everything he said but they knew he had come from God, indeed, was God himself. They were scared that Jesus' enemies wanted him dead. They could see that Jesus was very sad and troubled too. His closest friends had been with him when he had been praying in the vineyard and when he was arrested. He had asked them to stay awake to comfort him but they were so tired they kept falling asleep. One of them tried to stop the soldiers from taking Jesus away but Jesus told him off. And in the end, they all ran away. All of them! (*Turn the chair round.*) Emphasise just how much they wanted to follow Jesus.

Roman soldiers

The religious leaders thought there was enough evidence to persuade the Roman authorities to put Jesus to death. The Roman governor, called Pilate, being a rather weak man, agreed with the religious leaders. He gave orders for the Roman soldiers to take Jesus away and along with two other criminals, nail Jesus to a cross. (*Remove the SOLDIERS cloth.*) They whipped him then put a crown of thorns on his head, pretending that he was a king. They spat on him, hit him on the head, and then led him to a place called Golgatha, outside the city of Jerusalem. They nailed him to a cross of wood and hoisted the cross vertically. So Jesus hung there. They were just doing their job. (*Turn the chair round.*)

The crowds

Crowds of people gathered to watch what happened as Jesus died. (*Remove the CROWD cloth.*) These crowds had listened to Jesus talking to them about God, answering their questions, healing sick people, performing other miracles. But they were a bit like the mourning musicians in the story of girl who died. They were not really interested in following Jesus. Instead they shouted that if Jesus was as powerful as he said he was, he could surely rescue himself from dying on the cross. The religious leaders said the same! (*Turn the chair round.*)

God the Father

How lonely Jesus was. The pain was awful. He knew that God his Father loved him. (*Remove the GOD THE FATHER cloth.*) Remember that only the night before, Jesus had had this long and painful conversation with God. But the worst part of his suffering was that he knew that God was soon going to turn his back on Jesus too.

PHOTOCOPIABLE PAGE

PHASE 5

73

You see, in dying this unfair death, on the cross, all the blame for the ways people disobey God was placed upon Jesus. He was blamed for the wrong things that you and I do, even though he had done nothing wrong himself. When God the Father looked at Jesus on the cross, he could not tolerate what he saw there. It is hard for us to understand, but God turned away from Jesus. And Jesus knew that had happened. Just before he died, Jesus cried out to God and said, 'My God, my God, why have you deserted me?' And so Jesus died!

Summary using the props

Point to each chair back as you talk.

The religious leaders thought that they had got rid of Jesus. (They were in for a shock, because on the Sunday morning, Jesus came alive in a new way.) Remove this chair altogether.

Jesus' friends had run away and left him. One of them had betrayed him, one of them had let Jesus down and only one of them (John) was there when he died. But they had so wanted to follow him. After Jesus came alive again, they were to become Jesus' followers in ways they could never have expected. Jesus forgave them and they discovered just how much Jesus loved them.

The soldiers thought it was just their job to arrest someone and put them to death. But after Jesus died they had to admit that his death was different from any other – and they had seen a lot of people die! The officer in charge of the soldiers said, 'This man really was God's Son!' These soldiers may have found out more about following Jesus. Turn this chair sideways – they were undecided.

The crowds of people had many different responses – just like it is today. Some people were interested, wanting to know more and may have decided to follow Jesus. Others were interested in Jesus as a celebrity but did not want to know more. Turn this chair sideways – they were undecided.

God the Father had abandoned Jesus because Jesus had taken the blame for all the wrong in the world. But once he had died, the blame was wiped away. It was finished. He was victorious. Jesus could have saved himself but he chose not to. He came alive again. His relationship with God his Father was restored.

Response

We too can be a follower of Jesus, able to talk with God the Father. Or we can be like the religious leaders or some people in the crowd – just not interested. In the next session we will find out more

about what it meant for Jesus' friends that he had come alive again, what it means to be a follower of Jesus.

Invite children to think about what has been said. They could talk about this with their Engineers, or you could invite them to talk with an approachable leader who will be hanging around during the rest of the session. Have a booklet available which explains what it means to be a follower of Jesus. See the inside front cover for three recommended booklets – one for each age group. (You will want to remind the children of this just before they go to their Toolsheds.)

Day 5

Jesus' burial

Explain how Jesus was buried: Jesus died on a Friday afternoon. His body was wrapped up in a clean linen cloth and put in a cave which had been carved out of the solid rock to make a burial place for a man called Joseph who came from a town called Arimathea. Joseph had gone to the Roman authorities (who had put Jesus to death) to ask for permission to take Jesus' body away for burial. A large stone was rolled over the entrance to the tomb, so that no one could come to steal the body. Mary Magdalene and another friend of Jesus who was also called Mary sat close by and watched what was happening.

Toy shield

On the Saturday the Romans gave permission for the religious authorities to put some of their soldiers by the tomb to make sure no one stole Jesus' body. You may wonder what they were worried about! Jesus, before his death, had talked about coming back from the dead, and for once they were taking him seriously. They thought his followers might come to steal the body. *Take the shield out of the bag and talk about what other equipment soldiers use.* So the soldiers were stationed by the tomb, all that day and all through the night.

Ear plugs/muffs

Early Sunday morning, very early, just as it was getting light, Mary Magdalene and the other woman called Mary went to look at the tomb. Suddenly there was an earthquake, so loud, so scary that the women clung to each other. *Take out the ear muffs/plugs.* They didn't have ear muffs/plugs in those days and actually in an earthquake nothing can hide the sound or cover up the shaking. But these muffs/plugs are a reminder of what happened. (This was the second time that the earth had shaken that weekend. There had been an earthquake just after Jesus died.)

Sunglasses

The women were in for an even bigger shock for before their eyes an angel dropped down from the sky, pushed the stone away that was guarding the entrance to the tomb and sat down on it! The angel was so bright and dazzling and his clothes were brilliant white. *Take out the sunglasses*. They did not have sunglasses in those days but it would have been a help for the two women if they had had them. It must have hurt their eyes to look at this bright angel.

Sunglasses certainly might have helped the soldiers. They took one look at the angel and fell down to the ground. They were petrified which actually means 'turned to stone'. They lay there as though dead. *Produce the shield again and shake it with a trembling hand. Explain that the soldiers would have had no time to get their shields ready and their hands would have trembled too much for them to defend themselves!*

Running shoes

Then the angel began talking to the women. He told them four things:

1. Do not be afraid! (This was usually the first thing that angels said to people. It is a shock to meet an angel!)
2. Jesus is not here. Have a look for yourselves. The tomb is empty. (There was no body in the tomb despite the efforts of the religious authorities to make sure no one stole the body. It was gone!)
3. Jesus has risen from the dead, come alive again but with a new body, like his old one, but better.
4. Go quickly and tell Jesus' followers what I have told you. Jesus is going to Galilee where they will see him.

These two women were scared stiff but they were also very, very happy. Jesus was alive! *Take out the running shoes*. If they had running shoes in those days they would have put them on and raced to find Jesus' friends and followers to tell them. As it was, they just ran as fast as they could.

Sandals

But they did not get very far before they were met by …guess who?…Jesus! They knew it was him. He simply said, 'Hello!' just like he usually did. Amazing! But the women did not respond to him as they usually did with a cheerful, 'Hello there, Jesus!' Instead they fell to their knees and took hold of his feet. *Take out the sandals*. They now knew

he was God. He had come alive. And he was not a ghost. They clung onto his feet which felt just like any human being's feet. Jesus told them not to be afraid and then told them to go and tell his followers that he would see them in Galilee!

Response

What fantastic news to tell everyone! What a party Jesus' followers must have had, although it took some of them a bit of time to get used to the idea! Jesus had come alive and he is still alive, although no longer living on this earth. (At Sunday morning's service, you will hear the story of what he told his friends just before he went to heaven.) Once he was in heaven, the Holy Spirit came to earth in his place. The Holy Spirit is like Jesus everywhere, Jesus not limited to one place at one time, Jesus who can be with each one of us, wherever we are. Jesus who can be our friend – for ever and ever!

Invite children to talk about what it means to be a friend of Jesus for ever and ever with their Engineers, or with an approachable leader who will be hanging around during the rest of the session, if you appointed such a person for the previous session. Have a booklet available which explains what it means to be a follower of Jesus. See the inside front cover for three recommended booklets – one for each age group. (You might want to talk about this just before the children go to their Toolsheds.)

PHOTOCOPIABLE PAGE

PHASE 5

75

MEGA MAKERS! DRAMA

Professor Ventor's Miracle Matter-Maker

Cast

- **Professor Ian Ventor** – an inventor of Heath-Robinson style machines. (If played by a woman, call this character Professor Eve Entor.)
- **May Kamess** – the professor's assistant. She is generally useless around the workshop. (If played by a man, call this character Mike Amess.)
- **Remotely Operated Bionic Organic Trial** (or **ROBOT** for short) – the workshop automaton. Often the voice of reason in the midst of all the chaos. (Can be a woman or a man.) In his costume, it should be obvious he's a robot!
- **Dr Upton O'Good** – a rival inventor. Out to discover and copy what the Professor is working on. (Can be a woman or a man.)
- The apprentices (**Saw**, **Claw**, and **Bore**) – helpers in the professor's workshop. There is a different apprentice each day – these parts are ideal for younger helpers, or those not confident enough to take on a larger role. Dr Upton O'Good poses as one of the apprentices at the start of the week.

The scene

The action takes place in Professor Ventor's workshop. On the left of the stage is a large desk or workbench, on the right is a screen. The rest of the stage should be decorated with junk: inventions that never quite worked or have seen better days.

For most of the week, the professor's main super-invention, The Mechanical Miracle Matter-Maker is offstage. However, on Day 5, the machine is wheeled on. It should be quite an impressive prop, about six feet high with lots of dials, levers, tubes and buttons all over it. Tape two or three boxes on top of one other to get a good, big machine.

Sunday 1: introduction

Props: tablet, smartphone or clipboard and pen; a raisin

May: (*Walking on along the front of the stage.*) Professor! Professor! Where is he? (*To the children.*) Have you seen the professor? He's about this tall (*Indicates very low.*), this wide (*Stretches arms out wide.*) and always looks like this. (*Pulls a stupid face.*)

The professor walks on behind May. Some of the leaders encourage the children to shout 'He's behind you!' The professor ducks behind a desk.

May: Behind me? (*Turns round.*) There's no one there!

The professor gets up and walks back across the stage. The audience shouts 'He's behind you!' again. He goes behind a screen.

May: He's behind me? (*Turns round.*) Aw, stop teasing me! I wonder where he is.

The professor emerges, carrying a smartphone or tablet (or clipboard and pen). He stands behind May. The audience shouts 'He's behind you!' again.

May: Oh, I'm not falling for that again.

Professor: Hello May!

May screams in surprise and turns round.

Professor: Sorry, did I scare you? Our friends (*Indicates the children.*) did tell you that I was here. Now, have you got the results from the last test?

May: Well, that's what I came to tell you. I turned on the spud-o-peel-o-matic and it started belching out this horrible green smoke.

Professor: Smoke? Green? That's not meant to happen!

May: Well, that's what I thought. But I carried on anyway. I put the potatoes in for our tea, cos I love chips, and, well, it kind of exploded.

Professor: What? Did the potatoes survive?

May: Well, not exactly. This was all that was left. (*She holds up a raisin.*)

Professor: Oh well, back to the drawing board. (*To the audience.*) Hello everyone, I suppose we'd better introduce ourselves. My name is Professor Ian Ventor and this is my assistant, May Kamess. Somewhere around here is Remotely Operated Bionic Organic Trial, or ROBOT for short.

ROBOT: (*Entering.*) Good morning, Professor. How are you today?

Professor: He's the politest robot I know.

May: You don't know any other robots, Professor.

ROBOT: Professor, we need to go and prepare the Mechanical Miracle Matter-Maker for testing. (*Exits.*)

Professor: Of course, of course. Lead on. See you at Mega-Makers everyone!

May: Bye!

She rushes off pushing past the professor. He stops.

Professor: Look out for the dog-hair-knitting machine!

There is a loud crash from offstage.

May: (*Offstage.*) OW!

Professor: Oh dear! (*Exits.*)

Day 1 Welcoming the apprentices

Props: Broom, bucket of water (or small pieces of paper), cleaning trolley (or bucket of cleaning supplies), saw, claw, drill, handkerchief

May: (*Entering and waving at the children.*) Hi everyone! How are you? My name's May Kamess, I'm Professor Ian Ventor's assistant. I thought I'd get here early to try and impress the professor. We've got some new apprentices starting today and I don't want them to look better than me! Now, maybe I should start cleaning up. Then when the professor arrives, he'll be really impressed.

She starts to sweep and move things around. You will need to choreograph a slapstick section, where May knocks something off the workbench, knocks over a bucket, clatters into furniture and spreads chaos across the workshop. It should end with May in a heap in the middle of all the mess.

Professor: (*Entering.*) May! What's happened? What have you done to my magnificent new cheese-weaving machine? (*He points at a pile of junk that May has knocked over.*) Oh May, you certainly live up to your name.

May: (*Getting up.*) I'm sorry Professor, I really want to impress you with my cleaning skills.

Professor: Well, you've certainly made an impact on me. How are we ever going to clear this up?

ROBOT enters, pushing a cleaning trolley full of brooms, dustpans, mops etc (or carrying some cleaning equipment, if a trolley isn't feasible).

ROBOT: Let me help you. I have been programmed to clean up all kinds of mess, from accidents in workshops to accidents in farmyards. (*He starts clearing up.*)

May: (*Waving her hand in front of her nose.*) Poo! Stinky!

Professor: Thank you, ROBOT, at least one of my staff members is good at their job.

May: Oh Professor, that's not fair! I am good at my job! Well, mostly. Well, sometimes. Well, I did do that one thing well, once.

Professor: It's OK, May. Don't worry, I'm not going to fire you or anything. Now give ROBOT a hand.

May: ROBOT? What does ROBOT stand for?

ROBOT: Remotely Operated Bionic Organic Trial. The Professor built me from socks, vegetables and an old microwave.

May: Really? Can I cook my dinner in your tummy?

ROBOT: (*Looking at her sternly.*) No.

Professor: Stop the chatter, will you? I've got to enrol these new apprentices today. I've got four applicants: Saw, Claw, Bore and Dr Upton O'Good. Hmm, a doctor? He sounds a bit overqualified. ROBOT, bring them through please!

ROBOT: Yes, Professor. (*Exits and comes back with the four applicants. They form a line at the front of the stage.*) The new apprentices, Professor.

Professor: Welcome to my workshop. Can you let me know a little bit about yourselves?

Saw: (*Brandishing a saw.*) I'm Saw! I love to cut and chop things! (*Makes a sawing action with his saw.*)

Professor: (*Stepping back, a little bit nervous.*) Oh. I see. Er, lovely. (*Walks towards Claw.*)

Claw: (*Brandishing a mechanical claw.*) I'm Claw! I love to grab things and rip things apart. (*Waves the claw around violently.*)

Professor: (*Staggering back, more nervous now.*) Eek! Well, I suppose that could be useful. (*Walks towards Bore.*)

Bore: (*Brandishing a drill.*) I'm Bore! I love drilling holes! (*Operates the drill.*)

Professor: (*Mopping his brow with a handkerchief.*) Oh, my goodness! (*Walks towards Dr O'Good.*)

Dr O'Good: (*Offering to shake the professor's hand.*) Hello, I'm Upton O'Good. I love to steal other people's ideas and wreck their inventions.

Professor: What did you say?

Dr O'Good: (*Coughing.*) I mean I love to hear other people's ideas and make their inventions for them.

Professor: (*Unconvinced.*) Right… Well, none of you seem like the inventing type, but everyone's welcome here! You're all on the team!

Saw, Claw and Bore cheer and wave their tools around. Dr O'Good laughs an evil villain's laugh. May, who has been hindering ROBOT's tidying up during this, looks at Dr O'Good suspiciously.

Professor: I know, let's all celebrate with a nice cup of beetroot and blueberry tea!

They all exit, chattering to each other, apart from Dr O'Good.

Dr O'Good: Finally, I've gained access to Professor Ian Ventor's workshop. All his ideas will be mine! (*He laughs manically and exits.*)

mega makers! PHASE 5

Day 2: Machine disaster!

Props: a tablet or clipboard, a saw, a claw

Professor: (*Entering with a tablet or clipboard, followed by May.*) Now, the revisions to the Mechanical Miracle Matter-Maker. If we fix sections A, Q and double K on Saturday, then we can then fix sections F, V1 and P73 through D on Thursday. That means we have to fix my pants on Wednesday.

May laughs excitedly – she has played a joke on the professor.

Professor: May! Have you been changing my blue pants, I mean blueprints again?

May: (*Still sniggering.*) Sorry Professor.

Professor: It's a good job we've got the new apprentices to help; we'd never get anything done otherwise. Who's here today?

May: Saw and Claw are here. But they won't put their instruments down.

Professor: I didn't know they were musicians. What do they play? The accordion? The nose flute?

May: No! I mean I can't get them to put their saw or claw down!

Professor: Oh, that's a shame. I love an accordion and nose flute duet.

A loud droning noise comes from offstage. ROBOT enters.

Professor: Ah, they play the bagpipes! (*Starts to do a funny jig.*)

ROBOT: (*Entering, followed by Saw and Claw.*) Professor, the Mechanical Miracle Matter-Maker is making a great deal of noise.

May: The Mechanical Monocle Master-Mauler?

Professor: No, it's called—

Saw: (*Interrupting.*) The Masterful Matador Misty-Maker?

ROBOT: No, I said—

Claw: (*Interrupting.*) The Marvellous Manila Marker-Mailer?

Professor: No! I mean—

May: (*Interrupting.*) The Mendable Mandible Muddle-Minder?

Professor: (*Getting exasperated.*) No! I mean… I mean… Oh, I don't know what I mean now.

ROBOT: Professor! The machine is shaking quite badly, and bits have started to fall off it.

Professor: Oh dear, oh dear, oh dear. What are we going to do?

Saw: Don't worry, Professor, I'll fix it with my saw! (*Waves the saw around.*)

Claw: And I'll fix it with my claw! (*Waves the claw around.*)

Professor: NO!

Ignoring the professor, they both rush offstage. There is the sound of sawing and banging from offstage. Then a loud explosion. The droning continues.

Professor: Oh no, what have they done? May, go and see what's happened. (*May exits.*)

ROBOT: Professor, I compute that there is a 4% likelihood of them being able to fix the machine.

Professor: (*Putting his hands to his forehead.*) Oh no, my beautiful creation!

Saw and Claw run on in terror, shouting their lines as they enter.

Saw: Run for your lives!

Claw: Save yourselves!

Saw: Man the lifeboats!

Claw: Fire! Fire! Women and apprentices first!

May runs on during Claw's last line.

May: (*Like Scotty from Star Trek.*) SHE CANNAE TAKE ANY MORE, PROFESSOR!

The whole cast lurch from side to side, screaming as they go (just as they do in Star Trek when the Enterprise is attacked!). The offstage noises are very loud now. ROBOT fights his way over to the professor.

ROBOT: (*Shouting.*) I can fix it, Professor!

ROBOT staggers offstage. Suddenly all the noise stops. The people left onstage stop lurching around and screaming, May and the professor stand in various states of tiredness and relief, Saw and Claw collapse on each other. ROBOT comes back onstage.

Professor: (*Out of breath.*) That was brilliant! What did you do?

ROBOT: I just told it to stop.

May: (*Panting heavily.*) That's amazing! Did it just listen to you?

ROBOT: We're on the same wavelength. Literally.

May: Well, that's left me speechless that has. I mean, I don't know what to say – you stopped it just by telling it to stop. I've never heard anything like it. It's stolen the words right out of my mouth. I can't describe what has happened. If you were to ask me, I wouldn't be able to say anything!

Professor: May?

May: What?

Professor: Shut up. (*To ROBOT.*) Well done! Magnificent work ROBOT. I know, let's all have a nice cup of banana and chicken soup to celebrate!

They all exit, chatting excitedly, saying things such as 'Can I have croutons with mine?' and 'I don't like banana.'

Day 3: Power source

Props: Large roll of paper (could be a toilet roll), large paper plans set on the workbench, small detachable box fixed on the back of ROBOT's neck

Dr O'Good creeps on. He starts to poke around the workshop looking for something. If desired, leaders can encourage the children to boo.

Dr O'Good: I bet you'd forgotten about me, hadn't you? Well, I've been biding my time, keeping quiet and seeing what Professor Ventor has been up to. I have to say, ROBOT is an interesting invention. His power never seems to run out – he must be powered by some amazing batteries. I can't believe he was made from socks, vegetable peelings and an old microwave! I must try to get my hands on that power supply.

ROBOT: (*Entering, without the doctor noticing.*) Dr O'Good, you shouldn't be in here.

Dr O'Good: (*Surprised.*) ROBOT! How, er, good to, er, see you. I, er, was just looking for the professor.

Professor: (*Entering with May.*) Hello ROBOT, Doctor. We must get on with the refinements to the Mechanical Miracle Matter-Maker. ROBOT, have you got that calculation we did earlier?

ROBOT: Yes, Professor. Here it is.

ROBOT hands the professor a large roll of paper. Meanwhile the Doctor keeps poking around the workshop. He should end up crouched in such a position that, when the professor starts unrolling the paper, he gets covered by it.

Professor: (*Unravelling the roll of paper.*) Now, where's the answer… (*He keeps unrolling the paper.*) It's on here somewhere… (*He unrolls even more paper; Dr O'Good is now almost completely hidden by it.*) Ah here it is! Doctor, come and have a look at this. Doctor? Doctor? Where did he go?

Dr O'Good: (*Bursting out from under the paper.*) Yes, Professor?

The professor screams and drops the paper.

Professor: Oh, Doctor, you gave me such a fright! (*Looks down.*) Oh no, I've lost the calculation again!

ROBOT: Let me find it, Professor.

He bends down to look at the pile of paper. Dr O'Good gets a good look at the back of ROBOT's neck.

Dr O'Good: (*Excitedly.*) There it is!

Professor: Have you found the calculation, Doctor?

Dr O'Good: (*Flustered.*) Oh… no… er… I thought I had, er, but it was just a spider.

May: (*Shrieking.*) A spider? (*Leaps into the professor's arms.*) Where? Where?

Professor: (*Dropping May.*) Calm down May!

ROBOT: (*Picking up a part of the paper.*) Here it is, Professor.

Dr O'Good continues to examine the back of ROBOT's neck as he does this.

Professor: Come on May, you can help me input this calculation into the Mechanical Miracle Matter-Maker.

May: All right, but you promise me there's no spider?

Professor: Of course. (*Walking off with May.*) Except that giant one down there.

May screams and runs offstage.

Dr O'Good: (*Putting his arm round ROBOT and leading him across to the workbench.*) Er, ROBOT. Could you just tell me something about this invention here?

ROBOT: (*Bending to look at a set of plans on the bench.*) This llama locator?

Dr O'Good lunges for the back of ROBOT's neck and grabs a small box from his collar. ROBOT collapses onto the workbench.

Dr O'Good: (*Lifting up the box and laughing.*) Ha, ha, ha! I've got it! I've got it! Now, to copy this and make my own everlasting power source!

The professor and May come back onstage just as the doctor is shouting this.

Professor: Dr O'Good! What are you doing?

May: You're stealing ROBOT's power source? I knew it! I thought you were up to no good!

Dr O'Good: (*Slightly confused.*) I am up to no good. That's my name, Dr Upton O'Good.

May: (*Lunging towards the doctor.*) Give me that power pack back!

Dr O'Good: No!

May and the professor start chasing the doctor round the stage. After a couple of laps, they catch him, bring him to the floor and both sit on him.

May: (*Handing the power pack to the professor.*) Here you go. Power him back up again.

The professor walks over to ROBOT and puts the power back in his neck. ROBOT stands up.

ROBOT: Rebooting… wait one moment… Ah

PHASE 5

Professor! I think Dr O'Good is up to no good.

May: (*Pointing at the doctor, whom she is still sitting on.*) We know!

Professor: Come on May, ROBOT, let's get the doctor to the police! And to celebrate, let's all have a nice cup of my special tuna and tomato milkshake. Bye everyone!

They pick up the doctor and manhandle him offstage.

Day 4: Fixing the unfixable

Props: a piece of machinery, a penguin onesie (if you don't have a penguin one, use whatever you can find, and alter the description in the script), lots of shopping bags, a large hosepipe

Dr O'Good: (*Creeping on, to the booing of the children.*) Ha, ha! I bet you never thought you'd see me again. The professor shut me in the cleaning cupboard to wait for the police. But that stupid apprentice, Bore, drilled a hole through the door and broke the lock. So I escaped. (*Laughs manically, leaders should encourage the children to boo again.*) Oh shut up!

Professor: (*Shouted from offstage.*) May! Put that down! It's not a toy, it's a giraffe washing machine.

May: (*Offstage.*) It's OK, Professor, I know what I'm doin— ARRRGGGHHHH!

A loud watery hissing sound can be heard from offstage. The professor walks on, followed by a very wet May. During this offstage shouting, the doctor frantically searches round for a hiding place. He hides, but should still be in view of the audience. They should see that he's listening.

Professor: Well, you can't say I didn't warn you.

May: I'm soaked!

Professor: Well, giraffes require a lot of washing! Now, while we wait for the police to come, we've got some important work to do on the Mechanical Miracle Matter-Maker. Once that's done, we'll be finished and we'll be famous! Everyone will want a Mechanical Miracle Matter-Maker in their home.

May: Amazing! What do we need to do?

Professor: Well, we need to pop out and buy one or two parts – we need 50 clothes pegs, one giant hosepipe and a penguin onesie.

May: Why does the machine need a penguin onesie?

Professor: It doesn't. It's for me. You ruined my last one in the washing machine, remember? Come on, time to go shopping.

They both leave. Dr O'Good emerges from his hiding place.

Dr O'Good: They've almost finished! I can't let them become richer and more famous than me! (*Paces up and down.*) What can I do... what can I do... (*Pauses.*) There's only one thing for it. I'll have to sabotage the Mechanical Miracle Matter-Maker so that it breaks. (*The children boo.*) Oh be quiet. (*Rushes offstage.*)

The sound of hammering, banging, crashing and manic laughter comes from offstage. Then Dr O'Good comes back onstage holding a piece of machinery.

Dr O'Good: Right, that's that! I can't see that machine working again in a hurry. (*The children boo.*) I'm going, before that fool Ian Ventor comes back. See you soon, you big buffoons! (*Exits laughing.*)

The professor comes on, dressed in his new onesie and carrying a shopping bag. May follows, weighed down with shopping and a large hosepipe.

Professor: Come on, May, we need to get going! Then we can hold a press conference and let everyone know about our invention.

May: I'm going as fast as I can. I really don't think you needed to buy 54 pineapples or that industrial-sized food processor. (*Drops all the shopping on the floor.*)

Professor: Nonsense! How else am I going to supply all the reporters with enough of my speciality cocktail – pineapple and potted meat?

ROBOT: (*Entering.*) Professor! Professor! I have some bad news.

Professor: What? Have onesies gone out of fashion?

ROBOT: It's the Mechanical Miracle Matter-Maker. It's broken. There's a 98% probability that it's been sabotaged.

Professor and May: What? Who by?

The children should shout 'Dr O'Good'.

Professor: That villain? I thought we'd locked him up!

They rush off to see. Then they rush back on and start picking through the shopping.

Professor: We'll need the pegs, the hair dye, the electric whisk and that ham sandwich.

May picks up one of the shopping bags and rushes offstage with the Professor. There's the sound of loud hammering and banging offstage. ROBOT is still onstage, but looks offstage as if watching what they're doing. May and the professor come back onstage sadly.

Professor: It's impossible! We'll never fix it.

May: And I was going to be so famous! (*Starts to sob uncontrollably.*)

Professor: And I was going to help lots of people! (*Leans on May's shoulder and cries loudly.*)

ROBOT: Professor, there might be something I can do.

He goes offstage. Suddenly an electronic voice can be heard. May and the professor stop crying.

Voice: The Mechanical Miracle Matter-Maker is restarting. All systems are running and correct.

May rushes off to see what happened.

Professor: What? How is that possible?

May: (*Running back onstage.*) It's ROBOT. He's become part of the machine and put everything right!

Professor: Wow! I have to see this! Show me, May! And make me a pineapple and potted meat cocktail, I'll need to concentrate.

They run off.

Day 5: Today and for ever!

Props: the professor's machine

The professor and May come on, chatting.

May: I still can't believe what ROBOT did. He made himself part of the machine so that it would start working again.

Professor: I know! I really thought that the machine was ruined, but he restored everything!

May: Oh, hello everyone. You know, I don't think you've ever seen the professor's machine, have you?

Professor: Well, we should show you! Now, where are those apprentices? Saw, Claw, Bore! Where are you?

The apprentices tumble on and start to line up next to the professor. However, the last apprentice on crashes into the other two and they all fall over.

Professor: Careful! Gentlemen, I need you to bring on the machine so the boys and girls can see it.

Saw: Can I saw it?

Claw: Can I tear it up?

Bore: Can I drill a hole in it?

Professor: No! It's a very precious piece of machinery! Just go and get it.

They go off.

May: Do you think we'll be famous? Will I get on the cover of magazines and newspapers?

Professor: May, the fame and the money isn't important. What is important is the fact that we'll be helping people.

May: I suppose you're right. I would like to have my photo taken and look glamorous though.

There is a lot of noise and bickering from offstage as the apprentices bring on the machine. They should improvise things like 'A bit to the left!' 'Ow! It's on my foot!' and 'Back! Go back!' May and the professor look offstage, with pained expressions and hands over their eyes. They eventually work their way onstage with the machine.

Professor: Careful! Careful! Put it down here so the children can get a good look at it.

May: It's a brilliant machine, Professor, but I am sorry that we won't see ROBOT again. He was such a good friend, and he cleaned up after me too!

Professor: I know what you mean, May. He was the best of my inventions! Who'd have thought some socks, vegetable peelings and an old microwave could become such a useful ROBOT?!

If possible, the machine should start lighting up at this point. ROBOT's voice can be heard, but he cannot be seen, as he is part of the machine.

ROBOT: Thank you, Professor. That's very kind of you to say so.

All the people onstage scream. They look around to see where the voice has come from.

Saw: What was that?

Claw: Who was that?

Bore: Where did that voice come from?

ROBOT: It was me, ROBOT. I said it.

May: (*Looking around everywhere but the machine.*) ROBOT! Where are you? ROBOT! ROBOT!

ROBOT: I'm behind you.

Professor: (*Turning round.*) Where?

ROBOT: In the machine!

May and the professor rush to the machine to take a closer look.

May: Wow!

Professor: You're in the machine, but you can still talk?

ROBOT: Yes. It turns out that, by becoming part of the machine, my power supply will never run out and I will be around for ever, or at least, until someone decommissions this machine. And I can speak!

May: Amazing!

Saw, Claw and **Bore**: Cor!

ROBOT: And with my computer mind connected to the machine, I can make it work much better, so we can help more people.

Professor: The possibilities are endless. ROBOT, what's the best way of telling everyone about this.

ROBOT: A press conference will have a 67% effectiveness in telling everyone the good news.

May: That doesn't seem enough. We want 100% of people to hear about you, ROBOT.

Professor: Wait a minute; I think I've got it! What if we tell everyone we know, and then they tell everyone they know, and they tell everyone they know? If we keep going, then everyone will hear about this great machine!

ROBOT: Yes, that would be 53.874 times more effective, Professor.

May: Great! (*To the apprentices.*) Right, you guys – go and tell everyone you know about ROBOT.

Saw: OK! Hey, Claw, I've got something to tell you.

Claw: Really, that's funny, cos I've got something to tell you.

Bore: Hey, Saw, Claw, I've got something great to tell you about.

Saw: OK, Claw you go first.

Claw: Well, I think Bore should go first.

Bore: Really? Aw, thanks. That's really kind. You two have always been such good friends.

May has been watching this exchange, getting more and more annoyed.

May: Don't tell each other! You all know, you daft apprentices. Go and tell other people!

Saw, Claw, Bore: Oh! Right. (*They exit, chatting excitedly.*)

Professor: Right, now we need to tell people too! But first, I think we need a cup of gravy and grapefruit punch. What do you say May?

May: Er, OK. But let's get the machine in front of the web cam, so we can tell the world!

Both start to pick up the machine and carry it off.

Professor and **May:** Bye everyone!

Sunday 2: Two days later

Props: the professor's machine, the apprentices' instruments

Professor Ian Ventor and May Kamess come on, followed by Saw, Claw and Bore, carrying the machine.

Professor: Hello everyone! My name's Professor Ian Ventor and this is my assistant, May Kamess. And these are Saw, Claw and Bore.

Saw: I like to chop and saw!

Claw: I like to grip and tear!

Bore: I like to drill and bore!

Professor: (*Staring at them for a moment.*) I'm sorry about those three. They are a little bit obsessed with their own skills.

May: Professor! We should tell everyone the adventure we've had this week!

Professor: Oh yes! Well, let me show you the Mechanical Miracle Matter-Maker, which is going to help so many people. (*The machine lights up.*) And inside is my other great creation, ROBOT.

ROBOT: (*Voice only.*) Greetings everybody. I am ROBOT: Remotely Operated Bionic Organic Trial.

May: This week has been amazing! We had smoke and sabotage and apprentices and I got drenched and ROBOT fixed the machine and Dr Upton O'Good stole the power—

Professor: May, May, slow down. You're getting everything mixed up. Why don't you start at the beginning?

May: OK, sorry! Well, we got some new apprentices at the beginning of the week.

Saw, Claw and Bore cheer and say something like 'That's us!'

May: (*Looking slightly annoyed at them.*) Yes, but the evil Dr Upton O'Good was also among them – he was posing as an apprentice, but really he wanted to steal all the professor's secrets! Then the machine malfunctioned and almost blew up the workshop. After that Dr Upton O'Good tried to steal ROBOT's power supply so he could copy it, but we stopped him! So, in revenge, he sabotaged the machine, but ROBOT managed to fix it, by actually becoming part of the machine! We were very sad, cos we thought we'd never see him again, but it turns out that he is still there and can speak to us, even if we can't see him! (*Turns to the professor.*) How did I do?

Professor: I think you've got everything!

Saw: What are we going to do next, Professor? Can we saw something?

Claw: I want to grip something!

Bore: I want to drill a hole in something!

Professor: No, no, no! We're going to invent something new and useful. Isn't that right, May?

May: It certainly is! How about it, ROBOT?

ROBOT: That makes 98% logical sense!

All: Brilliant! Bye everyone! Goodbye!

They all exit, the apprentices carrying the machine off with them.

Inventor's sheet **1**

WIDER AND WIDER THE INVITATION TO FOLLOW JESUS

1 Where on the table?
Where will you place Matthew, four of Jesus' friends, Jesus and the Pharisees around this dining table? Draw a circle or small picture of each of them around this table. Now, where will you place yourself?

2 Spot the 8 differences in these two pictures of Jesus meeting Matthew the tax collector.

3 Think of five things that make you different from others in the Toolshed.

1 ....

2 ....

3 ....

4 ....

5 ....

Thank you, Jesus, that I am different from

.... because

....:

Thank you, Jesus, that you love everyone with all our differences.

Amen.

PHASE 5

mega makers! PHASE 5

Inventor's sheet **2**

DEEPER AND DEEPER THE TRUST IN JESUS

1 How did the disciples' feelings change throughout the story? These faces show how Jesus' friends felt when they first got into the boat and at the end. In each box, number these faces in the order that the disciples felt like this.

1 HAPPY **2** TIRED **3** ANXIOUS **4** WET **5** FRIGHTENED **6** SHOCKED **7** SAFE

2 Write or draw in the footprints one thing you want to thank Jesus for and one reason why it is a good thing to be a follower of Jesus. Then tell Jesus what you are thinking.

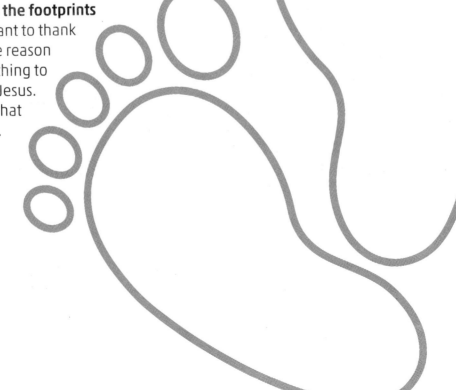

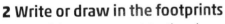

PHOTOCOPIABLE PAGE

Inventor's sheet **3**

STRONGER AND STRONGER THE POWER OF JESUS

1 Can you tell the story using these eight pictures?

2 Write or draw on this hand something you want to ask Jesus for.

· PHASE 5 ·

mega makers! *PHASE 5*

Inventor's sheet

GREATER AND GREATER THE LOVE OF JESUS

Religious leaders

Soldiers

Jesus' friends

1 How did each of these groups of people feel about Jesus? Colour the pictures.

People in the crowd

2 How many cross-shapes can you find? Jesus' friends are happy when they know that Jesus is alive again.

Inventor's sheet  5

FOR EVER AND EVER THE FRIENDSHIP WITH JESUS

1 How did the two women feel in each of these pictures?

A ....

B ....

C ....

D ....

E ....

2 Which piece of string leads to the picture where the two women meet Jesus? What did the women do after Jesus told them to tell the others?

3 Who can you talk to about Jesus? Write their name in the speech bubble and then ask Jesus to give you the best words to say.

• PHASE 5 •

Mega Makers!

THEME SONG

Andy and Wendy Green

Copyright © 2013 Andy and Wendy Green

MEGA MAKERS! THEME SONG CONTINUED

Andy and Wendy Green

Copyright © 2013 Andy and Wendy Green

PHASE 5

89

MEGA MAKERS! THEME SONG CONTINUED

Andy and Wendy Green

Love that longs to fill me up.... The Me-ga ma-chine makes things

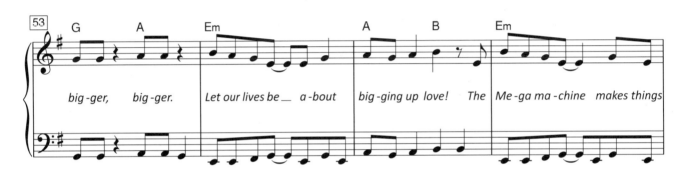

big-ger, big-ger. Let our lives be __ a-bout big-ging up love! The Me-ga ma-chine makes things

big-ger, big-ger. Let's keep on big-ging up God's great love! God's great love!

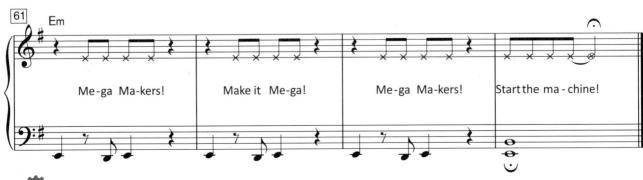

Me-ga Ma-kers! Make it Me-ga! Me-ga Ma-kers! Start the ma-chine!

Craft instructions

PAPER BOAT

① FRONT

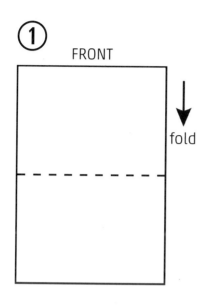

fold

② FRONT

fold — fold

fold

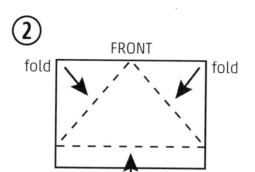

BACK

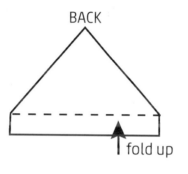

fold up

③

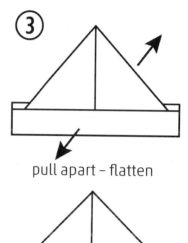

pull apart – flatten

④ FRONT

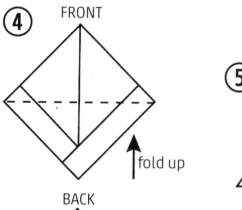

fold up

BACK

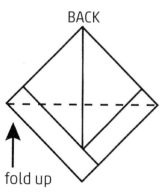

fold up

⑤

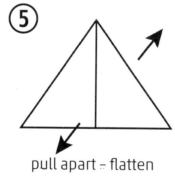

pull apart – flatten

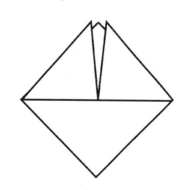

⑥ pull apart

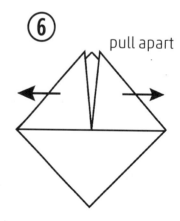

⑦ Boat!

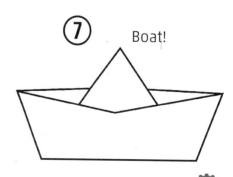

Extra resources

INVENTOR'S QUIZ

PHOTOCOPIABLE PAGE

INVENTOR	INVENTION	DATE
Steve Chen	**YouTube**	2005
Tony Fadell	**ipod**	2001
Ralph Baer	**Video games**	1967
Bette Nesmith Graham	**Correction fluid**	1958
Godtfred Kirk Christiansen	**Lego**	1955
Clarence Birdseye	**Frozen food**	1923
Mary Anderson	**Windscreen wipers**	1903
Thomas Alva Edison	**Light bulb**	1879
Jacob Fussell	**Mass-produced ice-cream**	1851
George Stephenson	**Passenger steam railway**	1825

ANSWERS

YouTube Steve Chen 2005; **ipod** Tony Fadell 2001; **Video games** Ralph Baer 1967; **Correction fluid** Bette Nesmith Graham 1958;
Lego Godtfred Kirk Christiansen 1955; **Frozen food** Clarence Birdseye 1923; **Windscreen wipers** Mary Anderson 1903;
Light bulb Thomas Alva Edison 1879; **Mass-produced ice-cream** Jacob Fussell 1851; **Passenger steam railway** George Stephenson 1825

WORKING WITH SPECIAL OR ADDITIONAL NEEDS

Value every child as an individual. Before the start, find out as much as possible about them – their likes and dislikes, strengths and limitations. Then you will know how best to include them and make them feel safe.

Prepare each session with a range of abilities in mind. Think carefully about working with abstract ideas. These may be misunderstood and taken literally! Have a range of craft ideas. Check that you do not give a child with learning difficulties a task that is appropriate for their reading age but inappropriate for their actual age. In other words, make sure that pictures and other aids are age-appropriate.

Give all children opportunities to join in activities. Some children with additional needs may have distinctive areas of interest or talents that you can respond to. As far as possible, keep children with disabilities with their own peer group.

If you have a child with a hearing impairment, make sure they sit near the front and that they can see the speaker's face clearly (not lit from behind). If a loop system is available, check that it is working for the child. Discussion in small groups can be hard for deaf children. Try to reduce background noise.

Pay attention to any medical needs noted on the registration form, particularly any medication they take. Keep a record of any medication given, initialled by the first-aider and another team member.

Designate leaders to work one-to-one with children with challenging behaviour. Where appropriate, set up a buddy system so that they work closely with a peer.

Expect good behaviour from all children, but be tolerant of unusual behaviour. For example, some children need to fiddle with something in their hands. 'Concentrators' can be bought from www. tangletoys.com

Ensure that all the children know what is planned for the day. Some children will benefit from a schedule in words or symbols. Give the children a five-minute countdown when an activity is about to finish. Some children find any change of activity very difficult.

WORKING WITH CHILDREN FROM OTHER FAITH BACKGROUNDS

We will not criticise, ridicule or belittle other religions.

We will not tell the children what their faith says, nor define it by what some of its adherents do.

We will not ask the children to say, sing or pray things that they do not believe, understand or that compromises their own faith.

We will value and affirm the positive aspects of the children's culture.

We will use music, artwork and methods that are culturally appropriate, for example Asian Christian music, pictures of people from a variety of backgrounds or single sex activities.

We will be open and honest in our presentation of what Christians believe.

We will be open and honest about the aims and content of our work with families, carers, teachers and other adults involved in their lives.

We will seek to build long-term friendships that are genuine and which have no hidden agendas.

We will relate to the children and young people within the context of their families and their families' belief system.

We are committed to the long term nature of the work, for the children now and the impact this could have on future generations.

Where children show a desire to follow Jesus we will discuss the issues surrounding such a course of action, particularly relating to honouring and obeying parents. We will be honest about the consequences following Jesus might have for them.

We will never suggest that the children keep things secret from their families or carers.

We seek to promote mutual respect between diverse groups and encourage community cohesion.

PHOTOCOPIABLE PAGE

PHASE 5

FOLLOWING UP **MEGA MAKERS!**

Ongoing maintenance

FOLLOW-UP IDEAS

During your holiday club week, you will more than likely make contact with children and families who have little or no regular contact with church. At **Meза Makers!** the children will have heard truths from the Bible, built positive relationships with your team and enjoyed being in community. It's a long time to wait until you do it all again next year! The following ideas aim to enable you to continue the important work you have begun and begin to disciple the children on a more regular basis, turning your holiday club ministry into a year-round ministry to children who may be currently outside the reach of your church.

Family ministry

It is vital to remember that children are part of families (however they might look) and that mission to the whole family is an essential part of passing on the stories and love of Jesus.

With a view to reaching the whole family, start inviting them to belong to the community, through events and in developing relationships. Once good relationships have been established, personal faith might be shared. This might take a long time to develop, but long-term commitment to children and families is essential. The ideas outlined below and those at www.exploretogether.org will provide you with some starting points for continuing the work with the children and for connecting with whole families.

Top Tips on Growing faith with families (SU, 978 1 84427 249 5, £2.99) is full of helpful advice if you're looking to start a family ministry.

Afternoon/evening activities

The **Mega Makers!** daily outlines provide enough material for one session: morning or afternoon. However, depending on the energy levels of your team and financial resources of your children/families/church, the holiday club lends itself to an optional extended programme, which could involve having a **Mega Makers!** room or event full of interesting facts and figures, images or videos about inventions and inventors.

You could run games and/or craft afternoons, using some of the more popular choices in **Mega Makers!**, together with options you didn't have time to try out during the club. You could even have some kind of sports competition! Events like these can be used to extend the **Mega Makers!** theme over the whole summer holidays if that's when you are running your club, with afternoon or evening events taking place in the weeks following the club.

One other idea to enhance the contact / maintain the relationship with the children who attend is to have a sleepover. You could do this (maybe with some fresh team!) on the last night of the club, perhaps after a family BBQ or, if you prefer, some months later when you could roll a Saturday night sleepover into a morning service and so invite and include those who were part of the holiday club but not regular church attendees.

Family reunion evening

A family reunion event, which could be held in a half-term following **Mega Makers!**, allows children to revisit the ideas and themes of the club and to show their families the kinds of thing they were involved in. Try to have as many of the **Mega Makers!** team available, as this will help children maintain the relationships they had at the club. Here is a suggested programme:

Clocking in

As the children arrive, they should go to their Toolsheds to catch up with each other. Play a game where you throw a dice and then talk about a specific topic assigned to the number you throw. Topics could include 'What I remember about **Mega Makers!**', 'What I did for the rest of my holidays' or 'What I like best about school'.

Meanwhile parents could either join in with the groups or have a drink in a cafe area, where photographs and pieces of artwork from the week are displayed. Make this environment as warm and welcoming as possible and ensure that a number of team members are available to talk to parents and welcome them as they arrive.

Inventor's workshop

Sing the **Mega Makers!** song and play one of the mega games from the club. Explain the stories and themes of each day in the club. You could retell the most popular story from the week too.

Games

Play some of the most popular games from **Mega Makers!**; you could even encourage the parents to take part!

Song and prayer

Choose a favourite song from the week to sing together, and then end with a prayer. Thank the parents for sending their children to the club and provide information about other up-and-coming events to be held at church.

Food

Share a simple meal together.

Midweek clubs

An ideal way to maintain contact with children is to hold a midweek club at your church or local primary school. Scripture Union publishes eye level resources, aimed at midweek clubs for primary age children, especially those with no church background. Go to www.scriptureunion. org.uk/2368.id and choose any eye level club as a follow-up to **Mega Makers!**

So Why God?, another eye level club, is suitable if you have children who are interested in knowing more about being a Christian. It takes questions children ask about following Jesus and helps them to come up with an answer. It also leads children in a sensitive way through the process of becoming a Christian. (See the inside front cover for details of *So Why God?*)

After school activities

Many schools run after-school activities so a weekly **Mega Makers!** club could become a fantastic follow-up to the holiday club, engaging with the children where they are already at – in school. In negotiation with the head teacher and key members of staff, the club would be able to provide creative art workshops for children, including the telling of a Bible story and some

opportunity for discussion. This will work best in small groups of no more than 12 children.

Mega Makers! days

Day events held throughout the year are good to maintain contact with holiday club children. These are effective when they coincide with a special time of the year: harvest, alternative Halloween, Christmas, new year, Valentine's Day, Easter. Here is a suggested programme:

- **Registration** and **Toolshed games**
- **Into the workshop** (with story, teaching, songs, games etc)
- **Games**
- **Break**
- **Small-group Bible exploration**
- **Lunch**
- **Construction**
- **Break**
- **Back to the workshop** (songs, Learn and remember verse, recap on story, interview)
- **Toolshed** time for interactive prayer and response time

It might also be possible to run additional **Mega Makers!** days when the local school has an inset day. Gathering a team may be more difficult as many will be at work, but it can be of real service to the community and parents who will need to be at work themselves.

Family days

The programme above need not be limited to children. There is something spiritual about families sharing and learning together. Ability is not necessary, and the children will enjoy helping other adults in activities with which they are comfortable. Therefore, one option is to hold a **Mega Makers!** day where you invite the family members of the children who attended the holiday club. (Parents, siblings, grandparents, aunts/uncles, godparents are all welcome!)

X:site

X:site is a children's event for 7- to 11-year-olds. Each event takes place every two months in towns, cities or whole areas and combines silly games, live music, videos, creative prayer, craft, drama, Bible stories and lots more so that everyone can learn about Jesus and have fun at the same time!

X:site is a great way to encourage children in your church by bringing them together with other children in their community – they will have such a good time that they will want to invite their friends to come too. **X:site** is organised in each area by a partnership of local churches; Scripture Union is really keen to see more **X:site** events happening around the country. With your help there could be one near you.

Check out our website and if you want to get involved get in touch with us. We would really love to hear from you!